Lizzy Hershberger
P.O. Box 14
Mabel, MN 55954
behindbluecurtains@gmail.com
www.lifebehindbluecurtains.com

NAUSET
PRESS
New York

Book and Cover Design by Nauset Press
Published by Nauset Press, LLC
Publishing contact: info@nausetpress.com

Cover image: Provided by the Author.
All interior photographs are provided by the Author.

ISBN-13: 978-1-962890-05-2

OVERLEAF: Lizzy Hershberger's diary

BEHIND
BLUE CURTAINS

A True Crime Memoir of an Amish Woman's Survival,
Escape, and Pursuit of Justice

By LIZZY HERSHBERGER

With MOLLY MAEVE EAGAN

Disclaimer

In order to protect the innocent people involved in this story, some names and identifying facts have been changed. The depictions of events, as well as verifiable facts, have been recalled and written accurately to the best of the author's ability. This is not an attempt to get revenge on any individual or the Amish church. It is not the author's intention to harm or disrespect any of the people depicted in the story or to incite conflict, but rather to educate and inspire change for future generations.

This memoir is based on the true life of Lizzy Hershberger. This book's descriptions are solely from her own lived experience and do not describe any other person's story or experiences. Some names, identifying characteristics, dialogue, and further details have been changed, added, or withheld. Any supposed likeness to any other persons, communities, or specific locations is unintentional.

Some traumatic events, emotional responses, and details were too difficult to write about. All memories were reconstructed based on personal diaries, in-depth interviews, conversations, letters, news articles, police reports, and court documents.

This memoir does not reflect all events, characters, and incidents. In an effort to be sensitive to readers, some of the more graphic details and other superfluous information were omitted.

It is the author's hope that each reader will learn something valuable from her story and use it to make a positive difference in someone else's life.

Ten percent of all book profits will be donated to support and educate
Plain people communities.

Dedication

This book is dedicated to my four children.

For all the Amish and Plain children, you are not alone.

Table of Contents

PROLOGUE
July 2018

I've never been inside the police station before. I park in the adjacent lot, so no one will see my car next to the jail, and step inside. A woman at the front desk takes my name, and the investigator for the Sheriff's Office, Captain John De-George, comes through a security door to take me back to his office. He clears off the folding chair across from his desk and motions for me to sit. My back is facing the holding cell, and I'm unable to shake the sight of four men sitting inside staring at me. John's suit and tie, neatly trimmed hair, and a reserved smile balance out his boyish face. He sits and folds his hands in his lap, waiting for me to speak. "I need to tell someone …" I stop, unable to finish, and cup my hands over my face to hide the coming tears. John gets up and closes the door. The din of the jail fades. I take a breath, determined not to waste his time. "I'm sorry," I say.

"It's okay," he says, setting a box of tissues in front of me. "Do you want to talk here? Or I can set you up with a victim's services advocate in a room where it's more private." The word "victim" hangs in the air, a word I'm not sure belongs to me. Then I remember hiding in the outhouse all those years ago—how cold and alone I felt. Surely, the word would belong to any other child in that situation.

"I'm okay now," I say, hesitantly. I try to measure how quickly I can get back to my car. I can still get up and say I'm in the wrong office. I can leave right now without saying a word. But instead I say, "I grew up Amish."

John picks up a legal pad and a pen and makes a note.

I think of my car again, worried that at any moment a neighbor will drive by, recognize it, and report me to the gossip mills. The thought of them keeps me rooted to my seat. "I left years ago," I continue. "I'm here to report the sexual abuse of Amish children."

"Amish children?" John asks. "Any particular child?"

I look down at my hands, noticing how worn they've become. "Yes."

John starts to write something, then stops. He clears his throat. "And who is the child?"

I sit up. I fight the urge to run. I have to look him in the eye for the words to come out. "The child is me."

* * * * *

The morning after I give my official report, I wake up before dawn. As I begin the day, I find myself remembering the diary. I haven't seen it in twenty-five years, but I have a hunch. I take the opportunity to bring a box of my daughter's old toys up to the attic, tiptoeing past my sleeping family to the trapdoor. As it creaks open, twilight filters in through the window, casting a path of shadows across the floor. I haul the box up the ladder and drop it at the top. A puff of dust plumes into a shaft of light and disappears. As it vanishes, my eyes settle on a box I haven't touched since it arrived two years ago. It contains *Datt*'s (Dad's) belongings, which came to me after his death. Dusty and bound with frayed tape, it looks ordinary. I know nothing about its contents, only that I never wanted to open it. But today, I crouch down beside it and touch the worn brown cardboard. The fragile tape breaks at the touch of my finger, as if promising to release something: an odor, or perhaps all Datt's secrets. The flaps tip open. Now, a small space separates me from my Datt's possessions. All I have to do is tug. I do, and there are his books and High German Bibles. I brush my fingers over the cool black leather. Datt. I can almost smell his smoky tobacco. He remained Swartzentruber Amish even after his wife and five children left, and he died alone. We had all sacrificed everything to escape, and he chose to stay behind. My first language is Amish, also known as Pennsylvania Dutch; my second language is English. Inside his books, the high German words remain foreign to me.

Among the tattered books, I notice something that doesn't belong: a small bound book with a cream-colored cover and a gold lock. Right away, I think, "Could this be *Mem*'s (Mom's) diary?" My stomach flutters, and I steady my hand as I open the cover. There, inside, is my mother's name written in her curly, nervous handwriting, not very different from my own at her age. The dates range from 1971 to 1974. I flip through the pages to July 26th, 1974, the day I, her first child, was born.

Fri. Baby born at 5 this morn. Wrote 4 cards & etc.

I flip the page.

Saturday, 7/27: Usual nite. Levi stopped by. Nice.

*Sunday, 7/29: Came home 10:30, Levi got the bed in, went to get the maude (*hired girl*) to help.*

I close the diary. No expressions of excitement or love over my birth. Her private thoughts about me were just as cold and emotionless as they were in real life. A wave of grief rolls through my body. I'm taken aback, silently scolding myself for the rush of self-indulgent tears. Mem's diary is only more proof of what I've always known: she never wanted me. I lay the book down and bury my head in my hands. I don't want my kids to hear me. I can still hear Mem's voice, an echo from the past, chiding me. "Stop your nonsense crying. Don't be such a baby," it says over and over again.

* * * * *

Rochelle is going back to college, to start her second year. She is the first of my children to leave home and the first in our family to graduate from high school and go to college. My husband, Titus, will drive her two-and-a-half hours away to River Falls. I surge with excitement for my daughter, wishing I could go with her. As an Amish girl, I was not allowed to go to school after eighth grade because the church considers formal education too worldly. I longed to see her dorm room, meet her roommate, and all the other things I'd missed out on. But one of us needs to stay with our three other kids.

Last night, Rochelle sat on her bed, scrolling through her phone while I rifled through a tangled pile of Bratz dolls and My Little Ponies. A plastic bin of collectible horses tipped over, spilling onto the rug. I gently chided her. "You have to get rid of some stuff, Rochelle. There's way too much to keep."

Rochelle kept scrolling. "You can get rid of all of it," she said. My heart dropped, and I wrapped my arms around the box. "It took years for you to collect these things. At least help me take the time to go through them."

She glanced up. "Mom, I was ten. Just give them away."

I sighed. "I'll put them in the attic. You might want them one day for your kids."

Rochelle looked up, surprised. "That's a long way off, Mom. I promise."

Our eyes met for a moment. Rochelle is nineteen with the whole world ahead of her. I thought of the early family portrait in our living room, taken when I was about her age. I already had a husband and a special needs baby, but compared to my Amish life, I was free. Still, I can't help but wonder what I might've become if I'd been raised English. Would I have gone to college?

As the sun rises just below the attic window, its light slowly spreads across the floor. It seems to be reaching for me, inviting me in. I'd already gotten Dusty out of bed and into his wheelchair, connected his feeding tube, and given him his meds. I knew I could count on his younger brother, DJ, entering his senior year in high school, to help out. I hesitate, titling my head to listen for signs that I'm needed downstairs. But I hear only the sound of laughing TV characters, followed by Dusty's giggles.

I step into the square of sunlight and sit down, holding the diary in my lap. The gloom of the dark, dusty attic disappears. I feel like a kid again, hiding from Datt so I could read one more chapter of a Danielle Steel novel. I open Mem's diary again, skimming the entries. They're short and to the point; comments on the weather, lists of chores, names of visitors. As I get to 1974, the year I was born, I stare down at the pages, aching for more. When I see familiar names, I rack my brain for their backstories, filling in gaps with stories told by Mem, Datt, my uncles and aunts, cousins, and neighbors, all of whom opened up as they got older. Back then, we were told sharing secrets was just passing on sin. No one was to be trusted outside of the community; and while the preachers, deacons, and bishops knew everyone's secrets they were not supposed to pass them on to anyone outside of the church. There is so much I don't know about Mem, so much I would never understand no matter what she wrote in her diary. Speckles of dust dance in the sheath of light around me. Mem's memories swirl around my own, merging then floating apart. The words in her diary begin to blur together, and I finally give up. I must put the story together myself. I close my eyes. I don't yet know what I'll find. I don't know if I want to remember.

PART I

I
Apple Creek, Ohio
November 1974

The train's gentle rocking kept me awake as it carried us away from Apple Creek, Ohio, toward Canton, Minnesota. Mem held me awkwardly, not so much to comfort me, but to show the English passengers what they were supposed to see: an impeccable Amish wife and mother. Living proof that our way was the Godly way, to be revered and protected at all costs.

Mem looked down at my angry face and pulled a cream-colored diary from the bag at her feet. She laid it on the seat next to me and stared out the window, but it was too dark to see anything past her reflection. She thought it just as well. She couldn't write about anything beyond the windows of the train, taking her safely away from the past. There was no looking back, no more fantasies about running away to California or becoming a singer. It was time to fulfill her higher duty to the *Gut Mun* (God). Most of her siblings never had a chance to leave their backyards, let alone travel 700 miles across five states to help establish a new community. The Swartzentruber were considered to be the most pious and godly order of the Amish.

November 30, 1974: *A new beginning*, Mem wrote in careful script. Her stepmother gave her the diary on her eighteenth birthday, although it was a requirement, not a gift. Many Amish girls received a diary to record their daily routines once they graduated eighth grade and their official training as wives and mothers began.

Mem had once dreamed of becoming a famous singer. She'd even snuck away to the movies and watched *The Sound of Music*, a major violation of the *Ordnung* (Amish rules). But all that was behind her now. The dreams as well as the social ostracizing. She could leave the old version of herself behind in Ohio—the woman who people pointed to in church as an example of what happened to girls who tried to leave the Amish.

Mem realized she was holding her breath and tried to relax. She reminded herself that love for her new husband and baby would surely flourish against the new Minnesota landscape.

I began to fuss again, and she paused, leaning in as she hushed. My tiny fist broke free of the blanket and landed on her cheek. Mem stifled a burst of frustration, touching the skin where my nails scraped her. She grabbed my fingers, wondering how a four-month-old baby could need so much maintenance. She looked down at my fingers. My nails were square-shaped, and their shape was nothing like hers or Datt's. They reminded her of someone else, a man who she needed to forget. Mem worried that I wouldn't quite fit into this new life she was building. As I began to cry, an English woman turned to look at us, and Mem stifled the urge to thrust me down on the seat beside her. Instead, she turned away to hide her tears. Mem picked up the pen and wrote: *They can make you do anything they want. Anything.*

My fussing continued. Mem stood up, balancing me on her shoulder, and walked across the aisle. Datt sat fast asleep, his feet propped up, and his head tilted back. He didn't take up much room. They called him 'Little Levi' because of his short height, but if it bothered him, he never let us know. His black, wide-brimmed hat sat beside him, big enough for its own seat. He would not put it back on until we had exited the train, as Amish etiquette required.

Mem allowed Datt another snore before kicking the knob of his ankle. His hat fell to the floor as he jolted awake. Sitting up slowly, he tossed the hat back into its seat and squinted at Mem in the dark. She held me in front of her like a platter, a silent command. He sat up and indulged in a yawn before reaching out to take me. My cries subsided as his long beard tickled my eyelashes and enveloped me in the soft, smoky scent of pipe tobacco. Mem handed him a bottle of formula.

"This artificial stuff is okay for the train, but not once we get to Minnesota," Datt said. "My Mem won't understand."

Mem bent over Datt to prevent other passengers from hearing her and whispered, "I told you she's allergic to my milk."

Datt groaned under his breath before he replied. "De Mem said no baby is allergic to her own Mem's milk. It must be something you ate."

Mem scoffed. "I'm eating exactly what the doctor told me to eat."

Datt paused and reached into the inside pocket of his coat, careful not to disturb me as he packed his pipe with a pinch of Prince Albert tobacco from a tin. Mem knew he would only continue the conversation after he'd taken his first puff. She reminded herself to be patient with her new husband.

After what seemed like forever to Mem, Datt spoke again. "You shouldn't be taking advice from the English doctors. Thank goodness *de* Mem is a midwife." He exhaled a slow, smooth plume of smoke. "She'll be like the mother you never had."

Mem crossed her arms and looked at the floor. "If I don't die in childbirth like my Mem." She watched me dozing off in Datt's arms, as if I might still snatch the life from her.

Datt reached out and tapped her shoulder, resting his hand there for only a moment before pulling away. "There, there," he said. "Get some rest. We just passed Madison. I'll wake you when we arrive in LaCrosse." Grateful, Mem nodded and walked back to her seat. Datt hummed softly, patting my back to the tune in his head until I drifted back to sleep in the crook of his shoulder.

Less than a year earlier, Mem had returned, unmarried and pregnant, from her attempt at "jumping the fence," or going non-Amish. Unlike more relaxed Amish churches, the Swartzentruber did not offer *Rumspringa*, or a break from the lifestyle. Little Levi was an old friend who'd had a crush on her since they were seventeen; and he offered to save her from the terrible consequences of her sins. As luck would have it, he already had plans to move away from the community that had branded her. Infighting among the bishop, preachers, and other elders in the Ohio Swartzentruber church district had been brewing for quite some time. Datt's parents found cheap, fruitful land in Minnesota near the Iowa border. Then they packed up their belongings in the middle of the night and told their son to meet them there after his wedding to this knocked-up Amish girl. Five of Datt's siblings, along with a few other families, followed. There were no goodbyes, no farewell parties. Disputes within the Amish community, instead of ending with a resolution, often ended with those who disagreed moving away. Datt had enticed Mem with stories about the dark, rich Minnesota soil, fresh water running from the wells, and rivers full of fish. "We would be one of the first Amish families to settle there," he told her. "This new world will be ours."

Datt had secured a job on an English farm, milking cows and feeding pigs, in exchange for our room and board. Our new landlords, Ted and his wife, Lita, came to pick us up at the train station. Mem happily handed me off to Lita, while Ted popped open the hood of his Suburban to show Datt the engine. Lita hurried me into the back seat, tucking my blanket more tightly around me. Mem covered her nose with one hand against the blast of gasoline. Once on the road, Lita held me close and made small talk as Mem stared out the window, watching the last bits of civilization disappear into secluded farmland.

Winter hung over the farm like an old, dark cloak. Mem scowled as she stepped out of the car and reluctantly took me from Lita. The small, dusty cottage sitting behind the main house seemed to stare blankly back at her. Datt watched her, amused. "It's only temporary, Mem," he said. "We'll have our own place soon."

Without bending her head, Mem looked down at the peeling paint and cobwebs on the steps. "Won't be soon enough!" she snapped. But Datt had already turned his attention back to gathering our belongings from the trunk.

* * * * *

December 22, 1974: *We were in de gma* (church) *at Dan C. H.'s. Lizzy stayed with Ted and Lita.*

"It's too cold to take the baby," Mem insisted, as she and Datt discussed going to *Gma* the following day. "I'll leave her with Lita. She'll be fine." Mem pouted as she lifted the heavy curtain aside and looked out the window at the snow.

"Bring an extra blanket. Mem and Datt will be there," he responded in his soft voice. "They won't approve."

"Lizzie can say what she wants about me," Mem shot back. Datt winced at hearing his wife call his mother by name. All the other women called their mothers-in-law "Mem." "I named our firstborn after her, didn't I?" Mem said over my cries as she shifted me nervously in her arms. "What more does she want?"

Datt stuck his hands in his pants pockets and looked down at the drafty floorboards. Mem laid me on the bed, took off her cap, and began unraveling the tight bun on top of her head. "You're so worried about the baby, you don't even care about me anymore." she paused and clutched at her heart.

"Of course, I care. You're my wife," Datt assured her. "I'll make sure you're both nice and warm tomorrow. Now let's get some sleep. Tomorrow is for the *Gut Mun.*"

Mem scowled as Datt put the matter behind him and got ready for bed. She glanced down at me, still fussing, then picked me up and carried me from the bedroom. She threw a log into the wood stove and dragged the rocking chair toward the heat. Sighing heavily, she sat down, hoping Datt could hear her suffering. I cried, even as the fire eased the chill still clinging to my bones. But the warmth couldn't ease Mem's discomfort. When Datt began to snore, she tied a scarf around my stomach and attached it to the chair to prevent me from rolling onto the floor. In the kitchen, she poured herself a glass of peppermint Schnapps, then rummaged through the pantry. She returned to me, holding up a bag of miniature colored marshmallows like a prize.

"Look what I found," she announced. "What color would you like? How about blue?" she popped the marshmallow into my mouth and watched as my bunched-up face relaxed. Relieved, Mem continued popping marshmallows in my mouth before I began crying again. She drank until the Schnapps bottle was empty and read from her secret stash of *True Story*! magazines.

* * * * *

Mem got her wish, and shortly after the New Year of 1975, Doddie and Mummy sold us five acres at the top of a hill on their 120-acre farm, and we moved into the small, wood frame, two-story house with a tin roof. The first floor was separated into four rooms: the mudroom, kitchen, living room, and Mem and Datt's bedroom. A cast-iron register allowed heat to rise through the floorboards. Even so, the upstairs was freezing cold in the winter and extremely hot in the summer. A single rotting window faced east. Next to the house, Datt built a small barn that housed our brown Swiss cow, Bessie, and the buggy horse, Rex. We had a sawmill where Datt used a diesel motor attached to a blade to cut logs and firewood, which he would then sell. Eventually, he built a shop where he repaired small engines and "tinkered around with useless inventions," according to Mem. A shed held chopped wood for the stoves. Swartzentruber Amish pride themselves on having the fewest modern conveniences among all the Amish. We were not allowed electricity, plumbing, or even toilet paper, so we kept a stack of catalogs in the outhouse. During winter, we used a bucket in our rooms at night, which we emptied into the ground or creeks come morning.

Mem busied herself with setting up her home, and from the start, it could never be clean enough. Her greatest pleasure seemed to be comparing the superior tidiness of her home to the others in her Amish community. She kept a can of air freshener by the door to blast into the path of anyone who came to the door. Tidiness served as a measure of our relationship to God. Music, movies, and television were strictly forbidden in Amish homes, and ours was no exception. Silence filled our lives, broken only by Mem's commands and the sounds of keeping house.

Each day, after Mem spent the day tidying and when there was nothing left to clean, Datt came in from the shop, sawdust from his pockets littering her newly-swept floors. The wind swirled in through the gaps around the doors and windows, shooting flakes across the floorboards and settling in the cracks. Mem stirred chunks of boiled potatoes and deer bologna over the wood stove as Datt dangled his latest invention in front of my curious face. Odds and ends of all shapes, textures, and sizes came clattering from his pockets onto the dinner table faster than Mem could bat them away. She refused to fill his bowl until the useless gadgets had been cleared away and his greasy hands washed clean. Before eating, they bowed their heads in silent prayer.

"What do you do out there all day while I slave away in this hovel that I'm supposed to make a home?" Mem asked, as Datt took his first bite. She stared at him while he chewed. "Well?" she snapped before he could interrupt with a second bite.

"I'm making some improvements to the hitch gear," he answered.

"Is that making us any money?" Mem asked, acting as though she already knew the answer.

"Oh, it could, maybe," Datt replied. Mem crossed her arms, waiting to hear more. But Datt just grinned at me across the table. He stayed in his chair long after Mem had cleaned up, smoking his pipe, drinking coffee, and looking out the window as if something amazing was about to happen. I sat on his lap and leaned my head against his chest, trying to see what he saw. But I saw nothing, only the familiar swath of orange sunset melting into the field and a silver moon rising in its place.

During our first Christmas on the *lut* (small farm), Datt brought home a surprise. They came barreling in the front door: two, pure-bred Eskimo Spitz dogs, as white as the snow that they splattered across Mem's black slippers. They slid across her clean floors, leaving streaks of mud in the wake of Mem's tirade. I loved them right away. We named them Mikey and Misty. After that first day Datt brought them home, Mem would no longer allow them in the house, I spent hours at the window, hiding behind the blue curtains, watching Mikey and Misty run free. I envied them.

One day, Datt went off to work, and Mem brought me down the hill to his parents' house. We called Datt's parents Mummy and Doddie. She planned to drop me off to be watched by Aunt Iva and Uncle Abe. Neither were married, and they both still lived with Mummy and Doddie. At the door, Aunt Iva picked me up with arms straight out in front of her, unsure how to hold me properly. Abe poked my belly button. I cried.

"She's fussy," Mem said. "But she needs to learn that she can't get her way all the time."

"What does she eat?" Aunt Iva asked, waving her brother away. "Abe, leave the baby alone."

Mem pointed to the supply of formula she'd set on their kitchen table. Aunt Iva eyed the bottles of chalky liquid. "Does Mummy know you're using formula?" she asked. Mem ignored her husband's sister. She had already given up on gaining Mummy's approval, knowing full well it was unattainable. Abe gasped as he watched Mem rub pink Chapstick over her lips and cheekbones. Another *Ordnung* broken. Mem didn't glance back as she rushed out the door to greet a man in a pickup truck turning into the driveway, hopped in and rode away.

Aunt Iva mumbled there was no sense in telling Datt. They never questioned Mem, because then they would have a moral obligation to report it to the preachers. And no one wanted to report to the preachers lest their own sins were noticed.

Aunt Iva had a Little Golden Books copy of *Cinderella*, one of the few (children's) books outside of the German Bible approved by the church to have at home. She sat on the day bed, put me in her lap, and read to me in her slow, unsure voice. Uncle Abe tied a napkin around his head to play Cinderella and made us laugh. The colorful illustrations popped off the pages in contrast to the simple, black and white lines of Amish life.

Whenever Mem stayed out all night, Mummy showed up the next day. If Datt put on a dress, bonnet, and a few pounds, he could have passed for his mother. She marched up the hill, stomped in, and bustled about, criticizing Mem for the color of her curtains, the number of store-bought items in the pantry, and the setup of her kitchen. Mem said nothing until Datt got home, then she called his mother 'Lizzie' to her face until Mummy left in a huff, and Datt went back to his shop.

II
Canton, MN
September 2017

*A*fter finding Mem's diary, I keep returning to the attic. I'd always thought of it as a dreary place, its dark corners stuffed with dusty old memories. But I begin to appreciate how the sun spills in through the curtain-less window, challenging the dark around it, and forming a cocoon of light just big enough for me. I buy a new journal and begin to write. At first, I try to fill in the blanks of Mem's diary, noting memories as they come to me. Many of the memories make me want to bolt up and busy myself with anything else. But something about the calm of the attic makes me feel like time has stopped just for me. And so, despite the discomfort, I remain still, appreciating the quiet scratch of my pen across the paper. No noise but the ones I create. Nobody telling me what to do or what to write. This time it will be my story.

III
Canton, MN
November 1975

Some bright morning when this life is over, I'll fly away ...

— ALBERT E. BRUMLEY, AS PERFORMED BY ALISON KRAUSS AND GILLIAN WELCH

ut Mun brought us a gift," Datt held the front door open, and Mem strolled in like a queen. Datt beamed at the bundle in her arms. It wriggled, and I clapped with anticipation, hoping that Mem would allow this new puppy into the house. As Mem began unwrapping the blanket, it let out a blood-curdling scream. I slapped my hands over my ears as I saw a tiny round red face making such a huge racket. Datt put his hand on my shoulder. "Here is your new sister, Royal." I had just started teetering through the house on my own and promptly ran away. Mummy whisked Mem away to the bedroom, closed the door, and the screams subsided. Why would *Gut Mun* bring us such a noisy gift? Royal wasn't at all like Mikey and Misty. She was fragile and demanding, and too little to play with me. With the mess and noise my new sister made, it didn't seem fair that my beloved dogs were banished to the shed each night while she got to sleep with Mem and Datt.

I often watched Mem put her face close to Royal's and make soft noises. She was more protective of Royal. Unlike me, my sister looked like Datt. She had his light complexion, strawberry blond hair, freckles, and thin lips. I had Mem's darker skin, pointy nose, and a stranger's bone structure. Royal was Mem's re-demption, proof I was the difficult one and that she was a good mother, despite all the talk.

"Royal is such a content, easy baby," Mem boasted to the women at *Gma*. "Lizzy rejected me when I tried nursing her, but Royal knew what to do right away." The neighbors nodded with approval but clucked their tongues with disapproval as soon as she walked away.

* * * * *

Tom was born three years later. Like Royal's arrival, there was no warning, no talk of conception, pregnancy, or birth. Datt teased Mem about her weight a little more than usual, but we never noticed a growing belly beneath her billowing dress and apron. Amish babies simply appeared. Royal and I, three and four years old respectively, moved into the small space on the second floor next to the attic. With no door and a sloping floor, I felt sure that I would roll out of bed and tumble down the steps during the night. As we grew up, Royal let me sleep next to the wall. "What if you roll out of bed?" I asked her.

"Then we'll be together at the bottom of the stairs, dead," Royal explained. That made me feel better.

Peeling blue wallpaper curled along the edges of the room, and a faded blue curtain hung across two nails, blocking the light. At night, we pushed it aside, pointing out patterns in the stars. Was the sky God's design? Or was it something else? We had just enough room to walk around the bed. A small dresser held our long, knee-high black socks, homemade bloomers, and two white handkerchiefs, each hand sewn with our initials. Mem also sewed our initials into the pockets just below the right hips of our matching dresses. We each had two everyday dresses, matching light blue *una reck* (under-dresses) that we wore underneath our dark dresses, and matching aprons. Royal and I could usually tell which outfits belonged to us without looking at the initials because I always managed to tear mine. I carelessly climbed fences and trees, unlike Royal, who was more careful with her things.

Mem kept our Sunday clothes, along with our black caps and bonnets, in her closet on the main floor. Two pairs of black ankle shoes (one for every day and one for Sundays) sat in a small closet under the stairs. Royal and I liked to hide out in the closet to get away from doing chores. We called it the dungeon. We couldn't hide too long, though, because Datt's shoes stank. If Mem caught us, she made us bend over a chair and whacked us with an old sewing machine belt. The number of whacks and where she landed them never seemed related to whatever we'd done to offend her, but it seemed tied more to how she was feeling that day. Datt preferred to spank us with a slab of wood, but it seemed more like an obligation to him. One smack or two across the behind, and he was done.

* * * * *

The *Ordnung* determined every aspect of our daily lives: from what we ate and drank, to what we wore, to how we made a living, as well as guiding our daily routines. Tuesday was for ironing and sewing. Saturday was for cleaning, baking, and everything else that needed to be completed before Sunday. We were not allowed to work on Sundays, except for regular chores, which were not considered work. My favorite time of the week was doing laundry on Monday and Friday mornings in the basement alongside a grinding Honda motor that powered an old Maytag washer. Mem laid Tom on a quilt thrown over the cold cement floor across from the fire pit, which heated a cast-iron kettle of water for the wash. Once she'd built a fire, it was Royal's job to watch Tom while I helped Mem load the clothes. The exhaust pipe stuck out of a small hole in the wall, and it carried fumes out of the house.

Mem loaded the clothes only after the water reached a dangerously hot temperature. She'd hand me the cloth diapers and let me feed them into the chugging wringer. I'd watch my tiny fingers reach closer and closer to the powerful wooden rollers that snatched the fabric away like teeth, waiting for Mem to grab me back at the last moment. I always felt scared that my thin arm would get sucked into the wringer. I think sometimes I intentionally got too close, so that Mem would pull me away. The Amish discouraged affection, and I liked the feeling of her hand on my arm, even briefly. Sometimes she'd set a pail upside down beside her, so I could stand on top and throw the bluing balls in the rinse water. They bounced colorfully about, dancing among the dreary clothes. These cleaning triumphs were dear to her. She constantly reminded me how lucky I was to even have a Mem, unlike her. All I knew about my maternal grandmother was how well she kept house and that she wouldn't have tolerated my fussiness.

But I also remember the light breaking through the small window and cas-cading over Mem's face. She'd begin to look lost in thought and far away. Then the humming began. Music was considered proud and indulgent, and I never even heard her whistle around Datt. But after a few hours of cleaning, cooking, and sewing, she would sing. I remember the heat of the fire in the wood stove, the smell of kerosene, the churn of the washtub. And Mem's beautiful voice, singing:

"When the shadows of this life have gone,

I'll fly away.

Like a bird from these prison walls I'll fly,

I'll fly away ...

No more cold iron shackles on my feet,

I'll fly away ...

When I die, Hallelujah by and by

I'll fly away."

IV
August 1979

One morning, Royal and I woke up and went downstairs to find Datt alone, sitting by the stove. The house was unusually quiet. We asked where Mem and baby Tom were. Rocking slowly back and forth, Datt stared down at the floor. Royal and I looked at each other, frightened, wondering if something terrible had happened. "Don't know," he replied finally, "Looks like she left on a trip."

Royal and I went into the kitchen, unsure what to do. I clutched Royal's hands. "She's left us," I whispered. I felt both scared and excited.

Royal snatched her hands away. "She wouldn't do that!"

Datt stood and came to the kitchen door. "I have to go to town, so stay inside the house and be quiet. Don't unlock the door for anyone." Amish people don't knock; they just open the door and enter other community member's homes as they please.

We hid in our room, peeking out from behind the curtains. We watched for Datt, as the sun dipped over the edge of the window and sank behind the trees. Finally, we heard a buggy in the driveway. "Is Datt home?" Royal asked.

I pushed aside the curtain. "Ya," I confirmed, relieved. "He's putting Rex back in the barn."

We ran down to the kitchen to meet him. His face looked grim. "Girls, pack two dresses. We're leaving tonight for Michigan."

Royal and I knew not to ask questions, so we quietly packed sandwiches to eat on the bus. I slept for most of the trip, but I woke up at sunrise to shake my sister awake. "*Goog nos*! Look outside!" We were just arriving in a big town with street lights and cars everywhere. "Datt, *vo sin mir*? Where are we?" I asked.

Datt took off his glasses and wiped them on his shirt. "Detroit," he said. "This is how a big city looks."

I had never seen so many lights, and I wondered where everyone was going in such a rush. It all looked so important. We got off at the next stop where Datt introduced us to our Uncle Arnold, the English man who married Mem's sister after her sister jumped the fence. Royal and I sat in the back seat of his pickup truck for the drive to their farm, excited to meet our English cousins. When we walked in, we saw Mem and baby Tom. Mem gave us a tight smile. Aunt Melissa took us right back outside, leaving Mem and Datt alone. Our cousins were in the barn playing with baby piglets the way Royal and I played with kittens. I'd never seen so many animals. In the living room, they had a television that kept us entertained for hours. I loved being away from home, free of chores, but after a few days, Datt and Mem brought us all back to Minnesota.

Mem blamed Datt for her disappearances. He was never home, she yelled, as Royal and I listened from our bedroom. It was true that Datt often stayed out late. But he insisted we needed the money he made in his spare time, working on engines for English neighbors. There was no resolution. Royal and I knew Mem had run off again whenever we came downstairs for breakfast and found her cousin, Cevilla, in the kitchen. Cevilla was like a younger version of Mem, except that she and Datt laughed and played cards together late into the night. I resented it when she tried to mother us and sent us to bed early so that she could stay up late with Datt. When Mem returned, we made sure the house looked perfect so she would want to stay. And we kept her secrets, to avoid hearing everyone in church talking about what a horrible mother she was.

Over time, Mem and Cevilla became great friends, and they soon decided Royal and I could look after Tom on our own. They began going off to see "the chiropractor," only to come back hours later, slurring, stumbling, and sick. With Datt often gone, I'd be tasked with carrying the ice cream bucket back and forth, cleaning up after Mem.

Royal and I continued our routine, learning to care for ourselves, our little brother, and the house. Each morning after chores, we took turns running errands for Mummy and Doddie: gathering the eggs in an old, rusty wire basket, cleaning them with a damp rag, and then putting them into egg cartons. We hung clothes to dry, took coffee out to Doddie in the butcher shop, and made trips across the wooden bridge that led to the spring well. In the summertime, we kept food from going bad without refrigerators or freezers by placing leftover food, milk, butter, and cream inside a large tub inside the creek. Whenever we ran errands for Mummy and Doddie, I dreaded seeing Aunt Iva and Uncle Abe. I never knew if I was going to see the nice Aunt Iva or the evil Aunt Iva, the fun Uncle Abe or the creepy Uncle Abe.

One day, I returned to Mummy's summer kitchen with butter from the creek and almost ran right into Aunt Iva. "What took you so long?" she snapped. The room was dark, the curtains pulled shut to keep the house cool.

"Where's Mummy?" I asked.

"Not here," Aunt Iva replied.

"When is she coming home?"

"None of your business!" she spat on the floor and turned back to her laundry. "It's chore time. You need to feed the animals."

When I didn't respond, she picked up a fly swatter and smacked the back of my head. I put the butter on the table and turned to go. She grabbed my ear and yanked me back, twisting it until I bent over.

"Did you hear me, stupid?"

I tried to nod, but my head felt frozen in place.

"Yes," I croaked.

"Why do you take so long to do one little task? Why are you so slow? Royal's not so slow."

"I don't know," I said.

She let go. "Because you're an idiot. Go feed the animals!" she kicked the slop bucket as if to slide it toward me, but instead it tipped over onto Mummy's floor. She jumped out of the way, fuming as some of the contents splattered onto her shoe. "See what you did? Mop it up before de Mummy gets home. You'll have to tell her you spilled the bucket, and you'll need to clean it up before feeding the calves. Come on, Uncle Abe is waiting for you in the cow barn. You better hope Mummy doesn't get home too soon."

As soon as I cleaned up the floor, I headed out to the barn. On the wall by the outside door, I changed into a milking apron: manure-stained and caked with dried milk. It was too big, so I wrapped the long strings around and around my tiny waist. Aunt Iva stood by the door, waiting. "Hurry up, fatty." I followed her through the swinging gate into the barnyard that led to the cow barn. Everyone took turns milking the twenty cows, but at age 5, my hands were still too little. So it was my job to bottle-feed the calves.

Uncle Abe stood just inside the doorway, half-hidden in the shadows, his thumbs hooked into his leather suspenders. I could see the sweat soaking through his blue shirt; his sweaty stench curled my nose. I gasped, knocking over a row of clean bottles. Most Amish in our area only bathed on Saturdays because of the time it took to heat water, and Uncle Abe smelled as if it was late Friday night. He removed his wrinkled straw hat, threw it on a hay bale, and slowly scratched his dark red, bowl-cut hair with dirty fingernails. I looked down, avoiding his eyes. A wad of chewing tobacco shifted in his mouth, cheek-to-cheek, side-to-side.

I loved the calves, and so I took my time feeding them, letting their tiny mouths nip my fingers. I could avoid Uncle Abe as long as I was tending the animals. I could feel him lurking behind me. Finally, he said, "Come with me. We can listen to the Mallard Duck."

In the neighboring horse barn, Uncle Abe had a hidden radio, which he told me to call the Mallard Duck. He knew I loved listening to music. He stepped out of the milk house and disappeared around the corner into the horse barn. The horse barn had a place where Uncle Abe could see anyone entering it without himself being seen. I took a step toward the horse barn, then stopped. I paused, unsure of what to do. Should I follow him and listen to music? Just then I felt Aunt Iva, bumping into my back. She stood right behind me, staring me down, a silent warning to keep walking. I followed Uncle Abe into the horse barn. He stood at the bottom of the ladder leading up to the hayloft. Aunt Iva poked my back. "Go on," she instructed. Her solid, heavy steps followed my timid taps up the rungs. When we reached the top, she pointed to the corner. "Sit down and stay there!" I obeyed and walked across the plank into the crawl space filled with loose straw.

The plank clattered as she yanked it away and out of reach. I was trapped. I had no idea why I was being punished. Because Aunt Iva spilled the bucket? Because I was slow and fat and lazy? Was this how all slow, fat, lazy children were punished? Or just me? Then she disappeared, taking the lantern and leaving me in the dark. The horse barn door groaned shut, and I scrunched into the corner, pulling my legs into my chest.

Hours must have passed. The stirring of mice in the hay and shifting of horses in their stalls became a comfort, reminding me I wasn't completely alone. I thought of the book 'nice' Aunt Iva had read to us: *Little Women.* I tried to pretend I was Jo, the main character, finding a rare moment away from her sisters to dream up stories. Not a scared, weak little girl getting into trouble. Maybe Aunt Iva would leave me there forever and tell Mem and Datt I'd run away, or maybe she would come back to beat me. A mouse wriggled through a gap in the window and disappeared. For the first time, I wished I was smaller so I could disappear, too.

Finally, the plank slammed down, snapping me back to reality and swirling bits of hay into my eyes. I could hear Uncle Abe snapping his suspenders. A knot of dread formed in my stomach, replacing the gnawing hunger. "I got some candy," he said. "Come on down, and I'll give you some." Suddenly, all I wanted to do was curl back into the corner. Uncle Abe chuckled. I strained my eyes to see him, but I only heard the plank creaking under the weight of his boots as he walked toward me. "Don't you want some candy?" He whispered. "It's right here in my pocket." The fabric of his pants scratched against my arm. "Just reach into my pocket. Don't worry." His shadow loomed above me. I knew I had to be polite and accept the candy, or something worse might happen. But as soon as I reached into his pocket, I felt something big and warm jump toward my fingers, and I knew there was no candy. Uncle Abe leaned over and whispered in my ear. "Never tell anyone what happened here, or more terrible things will be coming your way."

I never told, but more terrible things happened whenever Uncle Abe was around. He'd lure me into the horse barn with chores or into the hayloft with a new litter of kittens. He'd sidle up to me while milking or coax me into the hayloft with a wriggling ball of kittens in his lap. I'd hold out my hands, determined to rescue them from his grasp. No matter how hard I tried to avoid it, his arm would quickly snake around my waist and squeeze me against him, then slowly tighten until I couldn't move at all. His hand would disappear beneath my dress. Then came the discomfort, confusion, nausea, fear, and eventually disassociation. It was my first understanding that something terrible lay rotting just beneath the surface of my peaceful little world.

Afterwards, I would run all the way home. Often it was already late, and Royal would be in bed. "Where have you been?" she asked. I just shook my head and burrowed deep under the covers. "Lizzy," she whispered. "What's the matter with you?" I was afraid to tell her in case they put her in the hayloft, too. I wondered if they were right. Maybe I was lazy and slow. Maybe that's what happened to girls like me. I could still feel Uncle Abe's calloused fingers inside. Squeezing my legs together as tight as possible, my insides trembled, as if I could make the part of me that he touched disappear. Silent sobs racked my body as I clamped my lips shut so as not to make any noise. The last thing I needed was for Mem to come and scold me for crying. "What's wrong, Lizzy?" Royal whispered into my ear again and again. But I didn't tell her. I stayed silent for almost thirty years.

V
November 2017

*A*s autumn wanes, the attic stays warm long after the wood stove downstairs burns to ash. But winter clouds cast shadows through the window and dim my once sunny refuge. Rochelle will be coming home for Christmas break soon, and I can't wait to have her back safe and sound. Besides good grades, she hasn't reported much else, and I don't want to push too hard for answers. I worry that she's going to parties or drinking. I wonder if she appreciates the freedom that she has, and I hope she's being responsible. Part of me doesn't want to know. Mem didn't want to know, and so I never told her any of the things a mother should know. Rochelle could have been hurt long ago, and like Mem, I hadn't asked.

I move from the cramped attic down to the loft bed to be closer to the wide-open space of the living room and the visceral warmth of the wood stove. Closer to my kids and the present time. My pen stops, and a lump forms in my throat. I can't stop thinking about Rochelle and what I'll say to her when she comes home. In the corner of my mind, I can see Mem smirking, challenging me to do what she couldn't. She never liked me, I thought, because I reminded her of herself.

"I am not like you!" My voice startles me as it cracks the serene silence. A red cardinal resting on the ledge clatters against the window and flies away. Something inside me releases. I look down at the diary in my hands. I say it gently this time, "I am not like you." Then who am I? The idea startles me. I know who I am: a mother, a wife. The thought fizzles out, like a broken firecracker. The Amish girl in me says, "It's enough for any woman." My other voice, the woman who escaped twenty-eight years ago says, "I still don't know who I am."

VI
May 1980

R oyal and I liked to pretend we lived far away from the farm, away from Mem and Datt, Aunt Iva and Uncle Abe, the preachers, and the prying eyes of our Amish neighbors. When Mem sends us to feed the rabbits, we'd take off our mud boots and walk through the woods barefoot, picking wildflowers and twisting them into crowns to wear on top of our *kapps*. Sometimes, Suzanna, Karolynn, Rocky, and Atlee, the oldest of our thirteen Borntrager cousins, would meet us at the creek. We were all close in age, and as our chores became more demanding, we often got in trouble for playing together instead of tending to our work.

We crouched together at the edge of the creek, watching tadpoles and small minnows leap through the currents. We made paths across deep pockets of water with flat rocks so we could cross to the other side. Then, we'd gingerly step across our creations, careful not to let the hems of our long dresses touch the creek's surface. If we got water or mud on our clothes, Mem would spank us for being reckless. Safe on the other side, we'd run to the weeping willow at the edge of the field and hide beneath its low branches. We kept part of an old tea set there, collected flowers and wild berries, which we pretended were little cakes and filled the cups with water from the creek. Our guests were the baby raccoons, kittens, and squirrels that got sick or strayed too far from home. We nursed them back to health under the protection of the willow tree, so the community members wouldn't reprimand us for having pets.

In the barn, we kept a black cat, which I named Rebecca, and a gray cat, which Royal named Barbara. The neighbors complained they were a nuisance and called us *katza gnouchers* (cat-touchers). When Mem took her afternoon naps, we snuck them into the basement and played with them for hours. Mem didn't understand why it took us so long to get the laundry done, but we kept Rebecca and Barbara until they both died of old age.

On a Saturday, November 1980, Royal and I got up to find Cevilla in the kitchen instead of Mem. My heart sank. All she would say was that Datt had taken Mem to the hospital. Later that day, a neighbor drove Datt home in his jeep to tell us we had a new baby brother. Soon, Mem came home with Toby. "He looks just like Tom did as a baby," Royal said. I nodded in agreement. From that day on, our training as mothers began, and we each went about our routines carrying a baby on one hip. When our brothers got too big, we mothered our cousins and neighbors.

* * * * *

Never-ending upkeep on our home's blue curtains marked our loyalty to the Swartzentruber Amish. The color had to be exact, and strict rules on length, cut, and pleating fed many of the complaints between neighbors. One evening, two preachers arrived in a buggy in our driveway. We could hear Mikey and Misty barking.

"What now?" Mem banged the mop back into the mud room, sat Toby on the hickory rocking chair, and tied a scarf around his waist to keep him from falling. "Stay in the living room and watch your brother," she said, and went to the door. She stood quietly at the window as the men stepped off the buggy and then opened our door without knocking. Ezra Mast, the preacher, and Emery Zook, the deacon, stepped into our house.

"*Vegates*, Levi Clara," Preacher Mast spoke to my mother. Among the Amish, women are addressed by their husband's name, followed by their own. The preacher's stern lips perked up as he looked at Royal and me before settling back into a grim line. Mem lowered her chin slightly in deference and closed the door behind them.

"We've had some complaints from your neighbors." He waited for Mem's reaction, but none came, except she raised her head a little. He yanked on his wide-brimmed black hat and cleared his throat, waiting for us children to disappear. Royal and I ducked behind the living room door to eavesdrop and peek through the cracks.

"It's your curtains." The preacher waited.

Mem raised an eyebrow. "My curtains?"

"Yes, Levi Clara."

"What's wrong with them?"

Preacher Mast turned and looked at Deacon Zook, who shrugged.

"They're too thick and too dark."

"Light," Deacon Zook corrected him.

"That's what I meant," Preacher Mast shot back. "Naturally," he gestured to the windows, "anyone can see they're all wrong. The fabric is too thick, and it's the wrong shade of blue." He straightened up, looking proud of himself.

"I'm stuck with the fabric now. It's expensive," Mem argued.

"It is all of our responsibility to uphold the *Ordnung*. We must insist you replace them immediately."

Mem turned her back, which she wasn't supposed to do. "When I have the money for new fabric, I'll be happy to make them to your specifications. Maybe you can come with me to the store and help me pick them out."

Deacon Zook stepped forward. "I'm sure one of your neighbors will …"

"… tell you if I get it wrong again?" Mem grabbed the mop and began scrubbing the already clean floor. "I have work to do."

Preacher Mast sighed and ushered Deacon Zook to the door. "We'll let the Bishop know about our agreement today."

There were two more visits about the curtains before Mem yelled at Datt and got the money for the right material. It took another three more months for her to sew and put them up. The lighter fabric allowed outsiders to see through the windows, she complained. And why not have cornflower blue instead of the ugly navy dictated by the Bishop, who "couldn't tell the difference between cornflower blue and mud brown," she complained.

"We don't want any trouble," Datt said when Mem finished describing her ordeal.

Datt never had much to say when Mem complained. But he had plenty of comments for Royal and me, which he parsed out from his chair at the table while we bustled around him.

"Don't throw anything edible in the wood stove because it will make you poor."

"Don't be proud."

"Don't ever tell any adults about the feelings you have."

"And, God forbid, don't show your emotions."

"You learn to suck it up and move on," Datt said. "Don't act like an *aldi rins fee* (old heifer)," he repeated a dozen times a week.

* * * * *

"You're old enough to start school this fall," Datt said one day. I was six years old, excited and nervous. Mem let me help her make two new dresses and aprons. "If you're going to learn English, you can learn to make your own clothes," she said, as she sat me next to her at the sewing machine and handed me a needle and thread. I tried to poke the thread into the tiny opening of the needle, but it slid past. I tried again and again. Mem and Mummy made it look so easy. "I can't do it," I said.

"You can't sew if you can't thread a needle," she replied, cutting into the fabric.

"How do I do it?" I asked.

She put down the scissors and straightened out the pattern. "You keep trying until the thread goes through the hole." she looked over at the frayed tip of thread and motioned for me to continue. To finally thread the needle, it took nearly half a day, all my patience, and a few tears, for which Mem scolded me. Waiting for me to sew a straight line took more patience than Mem could manage. She let me practice on the buttons, telling me we would start over with curtains soon.

On my first day of school, Mem told me to put on my new dress. Datt ambled out of the bedroom, wiping sleep from his eyes, and smiled at my perfectly braided hair and new clothing. "Don't talk during class, listen to your teacher, and do what you're told," he said.

"Don't make any trouble," Mem added.

"Yes, Datt. Yes, Mem."

I walked all by myself across the lane and up the gravel road by our sawmill to the one-room schoolhouse for Amish children. I had a brand new, shiny black lunch bucket with my name on it, a new pencil box with eight jumbo crayons, and two lead pencils. As I stepped into the room, my bare feet left dusty prints on the floor. Teacher Bertha sat at a large desk in front of the blackboard. She glanced at me when I entered, then went back to her work. I looked around nervously then saw my cousin, Suzanna, walking towards me. "Lizzy!" she waved. "Put your lunch bucket on the shelf here." Suzanna, tall and slim with dark brown hair and eyes, was the oldest of the Borntrager family. "You can hang your bonnet next to mine on the hook here," she said. Suzanna's sister, Karolynn, and our neighbor, Wayne Troyer, were the only two classmates in my grade. Wayne greeted me by flicking the bow of my *kapp* strings. "Don't forget to straighten your *kapp*," he teased.

Karolynn reminded him that it was wrong to tease us girls, especially when we were just trying to chat and have some fun. "Us girls can't ride horses or do anything fun like you boys can."

Wayne's face turned red. Being a good neighbor was important to him. "Aw, I'm sorry," he said. "We can go sledding and ice skating as soon as the snow flies."

Bertha rang the school bell promptly at nine. Thirty-one students, from first through eighth grades, attended school in the same room. Once we were all seated at desks, she did roll call. Bertha shouted our names as if she stood before a vast congregation instead of a classroom of silent children. We all said, "Here," unless someone was absent. If no one answered, she called the name again, then asked a sibling or neighbor. "Why is he or she absent?" she demanded, as if the present student were personally accountable. "Farm chores" and "taking care of younger siblings" were the usual and acceptable answers. An explanation of "illness" would be followed by suspicious interrogation and copious notes recorded next to the missing child's name. We then sang two German hymns followed by reading. The language we spoke at home was not recorded in written form, and so all of our lessons were in English. We could speak only English during class and at recess; the rest of the time we could use our Amish words. Our English sounded like chickens squawking; we could barely understand each other.

The afternoon began with arithmetic followed by English and spelling. While the other grades stood around Bertha's desk for their lessons, I colored or laid my head on the desk, hiding behind the students in front of me. When Wayne got a better grade on a test, he challenged me with playful teasing, and it pushed me to do well. We became competitive in every subject, especially arithmetic. The language was only taught so that we could interact with English people during unavoidable business transactions. But I couldn't wait to learn to read the few books not banned by the church: *Little House on the Prairie*, *Tom Sawyer*, *The Boxcar Kids*. They were stacked on shelves in the schoolhouse, just out of reach.

* * * * *

The following fall, Royal got to come to school with me. I was thrilled to have my sister in the classroom. "Use *paffews* (peppers) today," Mem said as I started to pack our lunches. Royal went outside to feed Rex and the rabbits. I spread butter and slices of bell peppers over thick slices of homemade bread, then added an apple, a thermos of water, and a graham cracker each to our black tin pails. We walked to school barefoot along the edge of the short gravel road, our lunch buckets swinging by our sides. The crunch of dried leaves and grass beneath our feet along with the smell of wood smoke marked the familiar smell of autumn. Across the road, withered cornfields rustled in the cool breeze. We began walking faster as we approached the schoolhouse. Without a word, we raced the rest of the way to the door.

"First graders, come up for reading," Teacher Bertha announced. "The rest of you, keep quiet." We all sat in one room, each grade from first through eighth taking turns at her desk. They stood around her reciting from their books as the rest of us tried to stay still. Bertha expected us to keep our eyes forward and our mouths shut. Wayne blew a short puff of air from behind me, ruffling the hair at the base of my neck and making me laugh. Bertha's chair screeched across the floor as she stood up. "Order!" she yelled, then marched towards me. In a flash, she pulled a black leather strap from her pocket and used both hands to slam it across my back. "Get back to studying!" she snapped. The sting of the blow shot up my spine, but I knew that if I cried, she would only hit me again. I looked down at the open book on my desk as tears dropped onto the pages, blurring the words. When Wayne instinctively leaned toward me, Bertha grabbed his hair and wrenched it back. "Keep your eyes down!" she warned him. I closed my eyes, listening to warring voices in my head. One voice telling me she was mean, and the other voice telling me that we were the mean ones. I was ashamed to look at Royal. I was disappointed. I'd wanted her to be excited for school, at least for a little while.

A knock at the door snapped Bertha out of her rage, and she stuffed the strap back into her pocket. Her eyes widened, and her mouth relaxed. She tucked the loose ends of her hair back into her cap as she walked casually to the door. We all turned to see who was there. Two unfamiliar Amish men stood outside, but they spoke too quietly for us to hear. Then Bertha turned to us and told us to study and behave. "I'll be right back, students," she said in a sweet voice I'd never heard before. "Amos will be in charge while I step outside to talk with this man about an important matter." She closed the door behind her. Amos strolled over to her desk, sat back in her chair with his feet up on the desk, tipped his hat over his eyes, and fell asleep.

A half-hour passed before Bertha came back, smiling, her face flushed red. Her cap was crooked. Sweat had flattened the stray hair around the edges. I wondered if she'd been running. She turned around, and a few kids gasped. Wood chips speckled the back of her dress. It looked strange, but I wasn't sure what it meant until I looked over at Wayne. His face turned bright red, flashing a mischievous smile that he quickly covered with his hand. Suzanna, Karolynn, and I exchanged knowing glances, although I was still confused. The wood chips must have come from the shed, I thought, and Bertha must've been lying down in it. But why would she lay down in the shed? And what was the man doing? Maybe he was helping Bertha in the shed and she fell, I thought. But the look on Wayne's face told me it was something far more scandalous. Even so, we never spoke of it because to do so would be a sin in itself. Bertha turned and gave us a long, cold stare, then called the first-grade students again, forgetting they'd finished their lesson over an hour earlier.

* * * * *

"Girls, it's time to wash and braid your hair for *Gma*!" Mem yelled up the stairs. Royal and I were seven and eight years old. We helped each other undo our braids so Mem could wash our hair in the sink. I lay back on the cabinet, letting my hair hang down into the bowl. Mem rolled up a bath towel to place under my neck, then she poured a pitcher of warm water over my hair to rinse it. "You're done. Hop down, it's Royal's turn." She went to the pantry, grabbed the half-gallon jug of colored marshmallows, and set it on the kitchen table in front of me. I picked out a blue marshmallow and stuffed it in my mouth. When she finished washing Royal's hair, the painful braiding would begin while our hair was still wet. Oh, how my eyes would well up with tears from the tight braiding! She let me hold my yellow baby blanket during the ordeal. "Mem, how old do I have to be before I no longer need braids?" I asked, clenching my teeth.

"When you're thirteen and done with school," she replied.

I couldn't wait until the day I could put my hair up with long hair pins like Mem. To me, it looked like freedom. When the braids lay flat and my scalp turned red, she let me eat as many marshmallows as I wanted. I watched as she combed and pulled Royal's thick reddish-brown hair. Tears filled Royal's big blue eyes. I watched as Mem braided row after row, wondering if I looked as silly as my sister. Children were not allowed to look in a mirror as it would make us proud, according to the *Ordnung*.

The next day was Sunday. We got up early, ate breakfast, and got dressed. We each wore bloomers, under-dresses secured with safety pins, dark blue dresses and matching long white aprons. Then we helped put Tom into his pants and shirt and Toby into his dress, which Amish boys wear until they're potty trained. Datt didn't get up until Mem impatiently tapped her foot by their bedroom door with her high-heeled church shoe. She had already milked Bessie, made breakfast, washed the dishes, inspected all four of us in our *Gma* clothes, and put on her dark blue dress, white apron and cape. Finally, Datt stepped out of the bedroom, still buttoning up his dark blue pants. Mem grumbled under her breath about how late we'd be for *Gma* as she brought a singing kettle of hot water to the wash basin so Datt could shave. Datt brushed thick cream over his chin, then carefully shaved his jawline. Then he brushed his beard until it lay flat against his chest. Sunday would be the only day of the week I saw Datt brush his teeth. Mem lined us up by the door, crossed her arms, and sighed heavily, the sign she was getting increasingly impatient.

"I'm not a *Geauga* Andy who thinks they gotta' be the first people to arrive at church," Datt said. He leisurely walked past us out to the barn to harness Rex to the buggy. Mem held Toby on the front seat leaving just enough room for Datt. Royal and I sat stood right behind the seat with Tom sandwiched between us. Datt picked up the reins. "Giddy-up Rex," he called. Then we started down the road to David Harvey's house for *Gma*. As usual, we were the last family to arrive. "Whoa!" said Datt, as he pulled back the reins. Mem stepped down with Toby on one hip, the diaper basket on the other. Royal and I jumped from the back end of the buggy, our bare feet leaving patterns in the dust.

Inside, Mem, Royal and I took off our bonnets and set them down on a table covered with identical bonnets, then headed into the kitchen to sit next to the women with children. Men sat on one side of the living room while older women and unmarried girls sat opposite on long wooden benches. A procession of ministers preached in high German, which Royal and I couldn't yet understand, so Mem let us play quietly with small clothespins and rubber rings she kept in her pockets. Even though I was too young to understand the words, I knew I was supposed to fear this God. I imagined him sitting at His throne watching my every move. Like Paul Bunyan, He stood ten feet tall with a club or an axe on his shoulder ready to strike if I disobeyed my parents, elders, or the church. I had to keep my feelings in check. After all, thoughts could lead to actions, and He might strike my family or me for those, too.

After a four-hour service, the women served soup made from heated milk, browned butter, beans, and chunks of homemade bread, along with pickles, red beets, jelly, homemade peanut butter or honey, and more bread. Royal and I stuffed ourselves, then wandered outside, away from the prying eyes of our neighbors where we could talk. The woodshed door banged open behind us, and we both jumped. "Who is it?" Royal asked.

"Menno Harvey," I said. He was married to one of Mem's cousins in the same church district.

"Hey, little Levi's girls," Harvey called out. "Sneaking away so soon?"

"Na," I answered and clasped Royal's hand, then turned to go. She gasped. I looked back at her shocked face, then followed her eyes. Harvey still stood by the shed, his crotch hanging out of his homemade pants.

"Come, we're going back to the house," I said. We ran as fast as we could back to the house and stayed there.

* * * * *

One weekend, Mem decided it would be a good idea to let me experience non-Amish life. She arranged for me to stay overnight at the home of her English friend who lived in town. This was against the *Ordnung*, but by now I was used to breaking the rules. Mem dropped me off in the buggy and told me to remember I represented the Amish church and to be a good girl. I was excited to see how the rest of the world lived, but I was surprised at how noisy their home was. The Jefferson's pantry, which they called "the fridge," made a loud humming sound. Vehicles buzzed by on the highway just outside the house, and the TV chattered away. Life-sized dolls filled the living room, sitting in high chairs, rocking chairs, and on wooden potties. I was overwhelmed by all the glass eyes looking at me.

"Lizzy, come here," Darlene Jefferson said. She led me to their indoor bathroom and handed me a pink nightgown to wear. Warm water and bubbles filled the tub with the smell of strawberries. I threw my Amish clothes on the floor and slipped into the bath. I leaned back and closed my eyes. "This would be so nice to have every day," my bad girl voice whispered. The good girl voice interrupted. "Nice things are too worldly for you. God is watching." I slid further underneath the bubbles.

Darlene knocked on the door too soon. I got out and dried off with the most luscious, fluffy towel and put on the soft, satin nightgown. My long braids hung free down my back. Without my night-kapp and Amish dress, the good girl in me felt naked, the bad girl felt free. She led me to the bedroom, which was furnished with a huge, fluffy bed covered with a pink comforter and matching pillows. "You can sleep in here all by yourself," she said. "I'll sleep downstairs in the guest bedroom."

She held up a camera. "Now sit in the middle of the bed and smile so I can take a picture of you." I did what she asked even though Mem had told me never to pose for photographs. As soon as she said goodnight and went downstairs, her husband popped his head in the door. His smile reminded me of Uncle Abe, and I covered myself with the comforter. "You're looking very pretty in pink," he whispered. "If you get scared, just come over to my room. I'm right next door."

I just nodded and waited for him to go away. There was no lock on the door, so I dragged the dresser over several inches to block it from opening unexpectedly. I realized then that the humming pantry, nightgown, blankets and dolls, the different clothes and different church, didn't change how men behaved. Even my bad girl voice was agreeing with my good girl voice that night: "Even if I get scared, I will not go to his room." I fell asleep listening to the cars whizzing by in the distance.

* * * * *

Mem also let me spend time with my Amish friend, Rhoda, and her family. I loved being at their house. It was warm and welcoming in a way I'd never experienced. I watched, longingly, as her father surprised his wife with fresh cheese. She looked back at him in such a loving way. Rhoda's mother spoke gently to her daughters; her father joked with his sons. I kept thinking they were an ideal family, the kind of "Wonderful Amish" I read about in tourism magazines. Not like my broken family.

On one in-between Sunday, as I helped clean up after breakfast, Rhoda's father and oldest brother sat at the table, hunched over an Amish Bible. Her dad held a pencil in one hand, marking some words and underlining others. I was shocked. Datt always admonished us about respecting this book: "The Bible is to stay in the desk at all times." And Mem reminded us not to write anything in its Heavenly pages. Rhoda saw me staring and motioned to follow her to the outhouse. "Why are you staring like that?" she asked. I walked past the outhouse to the creek before stopping to answer. Maybe they aren't a normal family, I thought.

Defacing the Bible was a bigger sin than having the wrong shade of blue fabric hanging from the windows. "What are they doing with the Bible out of the desk?" I asked.

Rhoda looked bewildered. "What do you mean?"

"*Ordnung* is to keep the Bible in the desk."

"Well, they're studying it like they do every other Sunday," she said. "Datt is teaching my brother the meaning of some of the words in the Testament."

I felt so confused. "Is that allowed?"

"Of course," Rhoda said. "Aren't you going to learn to read the Bible?"

I was puzzled. "The preachers read from the Bible every other Sunday at church. Why would we want to read it again?"

Rhoda shrugged. "My Datt said we should learn to read it."

I couldn't believe what I was hearing. What father would tell his children to read God's word for themselves? This was another idea to tuck away on my list of evidence that my family might not be normal, even for Swartzentruber Amish. Rhoda's brothers also never came to their sisters' rooms during the night, as my Uncle Abe did when I had sleepovers at my grandparent's farm. Now I knew what a happy family looked like, and I never wanted to leave Rhoda's house.

VII
December 2017

*W*hen Rochelle comes home for Christmas break her freshman year of college, as soon as dinner is over and the dishes are put away, I pull her into the garage. It's the only place I feel safe talking without being overheard. It's here where I sit on a lawn chair, hunched over, talking to Royal on the phone about things I can't say to Titus. Rochelle crosses her arms, wondering if she's in trouble, and leans against Titus's truck, a reminder that her Dad will always have her back. If I ever have a problem with something she's done, her Dad will tell her it's okay. "You're not in trouble," I assure her. I hang my head, concentrating on an oil stain on the floor. "Has anyone ever hurt you, or touched you … inappropriately?" My voice sounds strange coming out of my mouth, forced and unnatural. It's not a voice I would trust, not a voice to whom I would tell the truth.

"Eww, Mom, no," she says.

I reach over and hug her, not wanting to let go. "Promise you'll tell me if anyone ever hurts you, and I promise I'll believe you."

"Okay, Mom," Rochelle insists and pulls away. Typical teenager, I think. I must look hesitant because she grabs my hand at the last moment to reassure me. "Don't worry. I promise."

I exhale, a sigh of relief. Rochelle truly has the world in front of her. She doesn't know what it's like to be violated. Her body is her own. She has two parents who love her and always will.

She wasn't raised in the shadow of the Amish church. Her grandparents had little influence. Datt died when she was fifteen. Mem lives sixteen miles away, but she's not allowed to be alone with the kids anymore. The one time she took them out, Rochelle reported that Grandma showed her how to switch the tags at Goodwill to get the lowest price. Then, several things went missing one year after Thanksgiving dinner. Even more irritating was how Mem used my flower pots as ashtrays. So, we didn't invite Grandma this year.

VIII
October 1983

God's punishment is coming!" Aunt Vera announced to Mem in early autumn, as Royal and I hovered nearby outside *Gma* one day. It seemed a harsh judgment for the conversation at hand, which was about not getting enough rain for our gardens and farms, typical talk for after *Gma* at this time of year. Vera's lips hardened, and she crossed her arms as if defending herself from whatever punishment was on its way. Autumn had settled in after a dry summer, but there was no relief in the forecast. The once lush, yellow fields of corn had withered to brown stumps suitable only for cheap cattle feed. Grapes that grew on the vines along our fences began to droop before they'd fully ripened. It had been the hottest summer any of us could remember. We stood in a tight circle looking up at the sky, as if by keeping watch we could prevent any harm. Vera continued. "It's not right. Someone should tell the preachers." Mem shushed her and glanced at Royal and me, so we pretended not to be eavesdropping. "The Bible says to leave room for the wrath of the *Gut Mun*," Mem said.

"The Bible says!" Vera snapped. "We're not supposed to read it for ourselves, so what do we know about what the Bible says except what they tell us."

Mem giggled, something I rarely heard her do anymore. She leaned in toward Vera and whispered, "Maybe *Gut Mun* says wives are the ones in charge."

Vera gasped. "He will punish you for even saying such a thing." Mem turned to make sure Royal and I weren't listening, her face hardening back into its usual stern expression.

On the following Thursday, October 13, our cousins, Karolynn and Atlee, were missing from school. As Bertha did roll call, I looked over at Suzanna, questioning her with my eyes. "Corn-husking," she whispered. Bertha looked up from her book, and we stopped talking. Our cousins took turns missing school during the fall harvest to help on the farm. We'd just finished arithmetic when a fire truck came flashing and wailing down the long lane going toward the Borntrager's farm. "Did you see that?" I whispered to Suzanna.

"What was it?" Suzanna asked.

"Fire trucks," Wayne said.

"*Shhh!*" Bertha hissed and put her hand on the black strap. We looked back at our books.

A few minutes later, two more trucks turned down the lane. We all leaned forward, trying to see. Bertha marched to the window and shut the blue curtains, blocking out the sun. Gloomy shadows fell over our desks. It was hard to concentrate. Through a corner of the curtain, I saw a shape that looked like Mem. I started to panic. "Why was Mem at the end of the lane?" A loud knock on the schoolhouse door broke the silence. Bertha walked to the door and stepped outside. "*Ver ist sell* (who is that)?" Wayne whispered.

"It looks like *de Lissie ihr Mem* (Lizzy's mom)," Suzanna said.

We took the opportunity to peek through the curtains. "A water tank!" Wayne sounded excited. "There must be a fire!"

We all looked at Suzanna. Hers was the only house in that direction. Bertha came back in, shut the door, and continued with the class like there was nothing unusual about fire trucks, water tanks, and multiple buggies going down the lane. I thought the school day would never end.

Knock, KNOCK, KNOCK. Someone else was at the door. It sounded more urgent, and for the first time Bertha showed concern as she walked to the door. It was Datt! I wondered if our sawmill was on fire. She stepped outside for only a few seconds before she returned to her desk. "Suzanna," she said soberly. "You and your brothers can go home now."

Suzanna's face turned white as she crammed her books back inside her desk and waited by the door for her brothers. They rushed out and down the long lane toward their house. Bertha stood by her desk with a cold blank stare on her face. "There has been a fire at the Borntrager home." Saying nothing more, she sat down and read aloud in German. But I wasn't paying attention. I just stared at the insides of the blue curtains, waiting for the next knock at the door. At the end of the school day, Bertha finally excused us. Royal and I grabbed our bonnets and ran home as fast as we could.

Mem stood on the porch, her face pale and drawn. In a flat voice I barely recognized, she described how Aunt Vera had gone to help Uncle Jonas in the cornfields and left Karolynn at home in charge of four-year old Lisbeth, three-year old Adea, two-year-old Henry, and seven-month-old Levi. Shortly after, Aunt Vera and Uncle Jonas saw smoke rising from the house. Jonas started running, jumping over corn stalks and fences. Vera hopped in the wagon with the corn picking rack still attached and yelled at the horses to "Git." On the way, she flagged down a delivery truck coming up the lane, pointing to the growing black cloud of smoke above her house, and the driver raced away to alert the fire department.

When she got to the house, Uncle Jonas and Karolynn had already gotten Henry and Levi out of the house. The boys were sitting together in the yard, while Jonas and Karolynn ran back and forth with buckets of water from the washhouse. Smoke poured from the top floor and down the stairs. Aunt Vera screamed for her girls. Uncle Jonas desperately tried to get up the stairs, but the fire was too intense. As soon as he threw water on the blazing steps, flames shot from beneath the door and reignited his path. Vera finally screamed to Karolynn to get Henry and Levi and to get everyone away from the house. Vera tried crawling up the steps through the fire, but her husband pulled her back. She knelt by the steps, crying out for her daughters, "Lisbeth! Adea!"

Jonas grabbed a ladder from the buggy shed and climbed up to the second-floor window. It wouldn't open, and he pounded his fists on the glass. As it smashed, huge gusts of smoke came blowing out. He could see Adea faintly through the glass on the floor inside. He grabbed her, carried her down the ladder, and lay her on the porch. Then he raced back up the ladder to find Lisbeth. There was too much smoke to see her at first. He called her name again and again, and just as he was giving up hope, he saw the bottom of her shoe beneath the bed. He squeezed underneath the frame, grabbed his daughter by the ankle, and dragged her out. He threw her over his shoulder, climbed back out the window, and started down the ladder. Uncle Elijah met him halfway up, carried Lisbeth the rest of the way down, and laid her down by her sister. Uncle Jonas collapsed, coughing and spitting out black muck. The little girls looked as though they were sleeping.

"But they weren't," Mem said. She let this sink in—our two little cousins dead. I'd never felt such heartache before. I tried to hold back tears, knowing Mem wanted to see a stiff upper lip. "This is a test of our strength," she said.

That evening, Mem said she felt ill. So Royal and I walked with Datt to the Borntrager house, and Mem stayed home with Tom and Toby.

"Why did God take the Borntrager girls?" Royal asked.

Datt took his time, making sure his pipe was lit before answering. "Maybe an accident," he said. "Maybe a warning of what *Gut Mun* is capable of when we live in sin."

"But Lisbeth and Adea were good, obedient girls," I cried, too forcefully for Datt's standards.

Datt looked down, a shadow of doubt crossing his face. "Maybe they were punished for someone else's sins."

I couldn't understand how *Gut Mun* could do such a thing, but I also knew that questioning His will was the biggest sin of all. Datt must be right. The fire was proof that anything could happen to us.

A neighbor had already replaced the smashed window, but it seemed to stare at us through the trees like an empty black eye. Suzanna stood on the porch with baby Andrew screaming on her hip. Karolynn stood still and quiet, her face gray and stunned. Datt went inside. Suzanna waited a few moments then motioned for Royal and me to follow her upstairs to the room she'd once shared with her sisters.

The lingering smell of smoke hit me as soon as we stepped inside. "Lisbeth and Adea had been hiding upstairs playing with matches," Suzanna said, as she rocked Levi back and forth to keep him calm. On the floor, the faint outlines of their little bodies remained. A wave of grief almost knocked me to the ground.

I could hardly breathe. Why did the *Gut Mun* need to take two little girls? Why them instead of me? I wasn't loved or needed like they were. We stood in silence, staring at the outlines, as if Lisbeth and Adea might reappear and get up to play with us. I looked over at Karolynn. Tears streamed down her face.

We went back downstairs and outside to get away from the smell. As soon as the funeral home brought the bodies back to the house, Suzanna ran back inside to hide in the corner of the living room. Our uncles' faces were grim beneath their hats as they carried Lisbeth and Adea, each covered with a white sheet, through the living room. They laid the tiny bodies on boards balanced on chairs in the main bedroom. Then we filed back out of the house, leaving a few people behind to take turns watching the two girls throughout the night, as dictated by the *Ordnung.*

The next morning, Mem and Datt were gone. Royal and I took care of our brothers until Datt returned to tell us that Mem was at the hospital with a new baby brother. "Another brother!" I thought. "Why does *Gut Mun* give Mem another child and take the Borntrager girls away?"

Royal and I put on our black dresses and matching aprons and went to the viewing. We lined up behind Datt and filed through the living room to shake hands with the family members. Datt sat down on a long bench with his brother's immediate family, while Royal and I sat with Suzanna and Karolynn. They both looked so sad and tired.

Mem arrived with our new brother, Daniel, and Myrtle, an English woman who drove us Amish around in a car whenever we couldn't take a buggy. Mem shook hands stiffly with each of her relatives, but Myrtle walked right up to Aunt Vera in the rocking chair, reached down, and wrapped her arms around her neck. Vera turned red and leaned back as far as she could. Royal and I looked at each other confused. We had never seen anyone do that to another person. Everyone else remained stiff, as if they, too, had lost life along with Adea and Lisbeth.

As Royal and I waited in the kitchen to leave, we heard Datt speaking in the kind of forced whisper that only draws attention. "This is *Gut Mun*'s punishment for Abe and Iva's sin!" We clamped our hands over our mouths and hunched down, listening. "*Gut Mun* is punishing them for what Abe and Iva did." Datt continued, his emotion building as he spoke. "A brother and sister sleeping together! *Gut Mun* took the little girls as a warning and punishment to all of us."

Royal and I crept away as fast as we could, not wanting to get caught having heard such a thing, as if the sin were contagious and might infect us just for listening. We crouched there together, unable to speak, until Mem came to find us.

The following day, we piled into the buggy and followed Adea and Lisbeth's bodies to the graveyard. I sat close to Royal, welcoming the warmth of her body next to mine. I held my breath, as if any moment I might sin and make her disappear. A long line of horses and buggies made their way slowly down the road, in front and behind us, as far as the eye could see. I'll never forget the cries of Aunt Vera, Mummy, and the cousins as they lowered the two small caskets into the ground. Behind us, the men sang in German. Their gruff voices cast a haunting melody beneath the sounds of the grieving family.

IX
July 1985

A few years after Lisbeth and Ada were buried, the Borntragers moved away, and new families began moving in. I'd watch from the buggy as the Greyhound bus came around the corner, crunching over the gravel. Amish children peeked out of every window. The bus door opened; the driver stepped out and unlatched the undercarriage stacked full of boxes and suitcases. One at a time, they stepped off the bus. As is the practice among the Amish, men stepped off the bus first, followed by the women carrying tired babies on their hips and the children trailing behind. Women were never allowed to walk in front of men.

* * * * *

When I turned eleven years old, Mem's brother, Joseph, moved to Canton with his family. Mem paced back and forth as his bus pulled in, trying to peer inside through the dim windows. I recognized him right away. He looked just as Mem had described. His wife, Maryann, stepped off the bus behind him, a baby in both arms. Six more children followed dutifully behind her. Mem walked toward them with her right hand extended. The families faced each other in two rows and shook hands until everyone had greeted each other. Uncle Joseph's family didn't have their own house yet, so they came to live with us. With four adults and eleven children, the next two weeks seemed endless. Datt's face, usually serene, paled at the sight of the three boys, Peter, James, and John, and three girls, Sarah, Delilah, and baby Anna, screaming and banging toys at the dinner table. Uncle Joseph chewed with his mouth open, breathing heavily with each bite. Meek Aunt Maryann shushed the children. At first, I thought this meant I could slack off and lean my elbow on the table or reach over my cousin's toy train for the butter instead of asking someone to pass it. But Datt's eye always caught me. His lips thinned, his eyebrows scrunched down, and I knew he disapproved.

Datt finally found them a run-down English pig farm just over six miles from our house on the east side of the Amish community. I was thrilled when they began packing. The bed Royal and I shared would feel luxurious without the extra bodies wriggling around and stealing blankets. But Mem said, "Don't be so quick to get rid of them. You're going to help get them settled in their new home."

"No way!" I shot back.

"Lizzy, don't talk back," Datt scolded from his rocking chair by the wood stove.

Mem continued, "It's time you learned to be a *maude*, and Uncle Joseph has gout. It hurts his hands and feet."

I groaned. "So that's why he sits in Datt's chair all day except for mealtimes and orders his son to put his socks and shoes on for him. I thought it was because he's too fat."

Datt banged on the arm of his chair. "Lizzy, that's enough! I won't have you talking about your uncle that way."

I packed up and left in Uncle Joseph's wagon, pouting, and looking back at the window over the bed that Royal would have all to herself. That was my introduction to becoming a *maude*, a live-in maid, cook, nanny, and day laborer, a job most Amish girls become familiar with at a young age. It was grueling work, seven days a week, for not much pay. The Amish are exempt from the federal school attendance law after the U.S. Supreme Court ruled in 1972 that the law violated their rights under the First Amendment, which guarantees freedom of religion. As Amish girls, we were expected to work at school and chores through eighth grade or the age of fourteen. Then we would serve as full-time *maudes* until finding Amish husbands.

Every day was repetitive: filled with screaming babies, dozens of dirty diapers, cooking, cleaning, ironing, laundry, dishes, gardening, and milking the cows by hand. Aunt Maryann was quiet, kind to me, and obedient to her husband. Uncle Joseph never helped with the children or housework, yet he always complained that nothing was done right. He yelled at me constantly.

"You're a horrible excuse for a hired girl! The *Gut Mun* hates children like you," he reminded me daily. Working for Uncle Joseph made me never want to marry and be an Amish wife. I would never be a "broodmare" and have babies every year. There had to be more to life than just reproducing.

* * * * *

The following summer, I turned twelve and went to work for Datt's brother, Emanuel, and his wife, Karoline. They had eleven children, and the oldest child was ten years old. They lived over six miles away in a new church district on the west side of Highway 21. Called West Dale, it had a less unruly reputation than our side of the highway, the East Dale. The bishop lived on the west side, so Mem said it wasn't so easy to break the rules. I found Aunt Karoline to be the ideal Amish woman. I never heard her yell at the children or saw her get angry like Mem. She never seemed anxious, and I enjoyed learning how to run a house from her. But without Royal to play with during chores, or Datt's company to look forward to at the end of the day, the constant work felt even more grueling. There was always a dirty diaper to be changed or a nose to be wiped. And I disliked sleeping alone, in a dark corner at the top of the stairs in their sweltering house.

Twice a day, I left the children in their cribs with full bottles and pacifiers to go milk the cows in the barn. It was my first experience milking two cows by myself, and I was horrible at it. I ended up squirting most of the milk onto myself instead of into the bucket. My apron was stiff and smelly with spoiled milk, and it made my nose wrinkle with disgust. Across the barn, a huge black bull stared at me from his pen, banging the ring in his nose on the water tank and rattling his long chain through the water pan. Although a lock secured the pen shut, I was terrified of this bull. I was dead certain he would break out of his pen and charge me.

Each morning, Aunt Karoline put out a box of generic-brand corn flakes, a plate of chocolate cake, and a quart jar of cow's milk straight from the barn. At sundown after chores, we often ate coffee sup, an Amish soup made with hot milk and instant coffee. Once a week, I got to walk to my neighbors' houses to gather a list of things they wanted from the Amish variety store. I enjoyed slowly walking away from the housework, screaming children, the milking, and the angry bull.

It was the only time I had to myself. Even in bed, after prayers, I felt God was watching and judging me for my transgressions.

* * * * *

Then I got my period. There had been no talk from Mem about menstruation, no books illustrating the insides of my body, no trip to the drugstore to buy supplies. I sat in the outhouse, crumpling stained wads of newspaper into balls so I could hide them in the woods. Mem's words crept into my head. Was this God's punishment for me? Was I bleeding to death in the outhouse? I pictured Mem finding my lifeless body and collapsing with guilt over the sins she'd committed to cause my death.

But when I told Mem, she only said that I would have new rules to follow each month. Going barefoot was forbidden during "my time of the month." I still had to do chores, but no corn husking, strawberry picking, lawn mowing, hoeing, or weeding. Mummy warned me to be careful around Jim the Bull. "If he smells the blood, he might attack you," she warned. It made walking past the cattle in the pasture even more nerve-racking. While I didn't look forward to the monthly cramps or the teasing from other girls whenever I wore socks and shoes, I accepted it as one more punishment for being born a girl.

* * * * *

The summer I turned twelve, Mem, Royal, and my brothers fell suddenly sick. Nausea kept them in bed for two weeks. Datt and I were the only ones not affected by the mysterious illness. I hurried back and forth from the kitchen to their rooms, caring for them with Mem's homemade flu remedies. Until one day, Datt said, "Something needs to change." He took them to the doctor, who asked Datt if they'd eaten anything unusual.

"Nothing out of the ordinary," Datt answered. "What's wrong?"

The doctor lowered his voice. "I believe they're being poisoned. It must be something they're consuming daily. You'd better take a look at your food supply."

Back at home, Mem frantically looked through the pantry and basement for anything rotten or expired, but she found nothing. Regardless, she threw much of it away. A few days later, my friend, Rhoda, came to our door. She looked behind her before stepping quickly inside. "Well," Mem said, waiting. "*Vas veit* (what is it)?"

"I helped do chores with Abe and Iva the other night," Rhoda whispered.

"Yes? Speak up," Mem insisted.

Rhoda hesitated at Mem's icy demeanor, then looked at my baby brother, pale and quiet, in her arms and continued. "Please don't tell them I was here. Iva showed me how she slipped pig vaccine into your milk jug. She and Abe were laughing because you had to take your children to the doctor. I can't live with the secret. I had to tell you." Then she let herself out and hurried away.

Mem stared out the window after the girl, her expression changing from shock to rage, as she put the pieces together. Once a year, Bessie the cow stopped producing milk when she was about to birth a calf. Each evening during that time, Royal and I took turns leaving an empty half-gallon jar at Doddie's milk house; we'd pick it up full of milk in the mornings. Bessie had just given birth. Cow's milk made Datt and me queasy. We rarely drank it, so we were the only ones who didn't get sick.

"Stay here!" Mem commanded and marched straight down to Mummy and Doddie's farm. When she returned, she said nothing more until Datt came home. "Your own sister tried to poison us!" she yelled.

"We don't know that," Datt protested.

Mem stomped her foot, cutting him off. "She practically admitted it. She told Mummy and Doddie if I kept talking about it, she would leave the Amish for good." She waited for Datt to respond. He stayed silent.

Mem's face turned red. "She can get away with anything as long as she threatens to leave! She can kill your children, but God forbid she runs away. Maybe I'll run away with your children. Would anyone care about that?"

Datt just sighed and packed his pipe. "We'll get our milk from the local store," he said.

We never picked up milk from Mummy and Doddie's again. But our beloved dogs, Mike and Misty had drunk the milk, and both became sick and died shortly after. Life went on as usual, and it was never mentioned again. I continued to wonder what other secrets Aunt Iva and Uncle Abe were keeping.

* * * * *

In the early fall of 1986, Datt and Uncle Abe cut lumber in the sawmill for a new hayloft on top of Doddie's cow barn. Royal, Tom, and I took turns helping. I loved being around the sawmill with Datt and the smell of fresh sawdust. When the lumber was ready, other Amish families came over to help, and Doddie threw a barn-raising frolic. Women and girls prepared and served the food.

Royal and I liked to sneak away from the kitchen and sit under a walnut tree to watch the first few timbers go up. We could hear Datt's voice: "Ready, set, up!" And right before our eyes, the men would raise the barn by hand. Long tables were set up under shade trees for the feast. The women prepared huge kettles of mashed potatoes, gravy, fried chicken, tapioca salads, pies, cakes, and home-canned peaches. Young girls waitressed, watching and refilling anything at risk of being empty. The men shoveled food into their mouths faster than we could refill their bowls. Cevilla, newly married to Datt's first cousin, now stood side by side with Mem, barking at us not to keep the men waiting. Every second took precious time away from building the barn, they reminded us. After lunch, I listened for the sound of hammers on tin, which meant they were finishing the roof and would soon be ready for dinner. By then, the air felt heavy and stank with sweat.

I was pouring lemonade when a boy looked up and grinned at me with the biggest buck teeth I ever saw. None of the men or boys ever acknowledged us when we were working. We appeared as we were supposed to: silent, obedient, seen but not heard. One of the other boys snickered, but Titus, the one who smiled at me, didn't seem to mind.

"You're welcome," I whispered and continued pouring, as the boys teased Titus for his kindness. Royal asked why I was blushing. I didn't know myself. Titus was four years older than me, and I had no experience with boys. But he had kind eyes like Datt. And he smiled at me.

Titus and his family had moved to Canton at the same time as Uncle Joseph and Aunt Maryann. I often saw him when I went shopping with Mem. Our parents became friends, as did our siblings and cousins, and we saw each other often. Titus was too shy to talk to me, but I felt safe when he was around. I knew he wouldn't flash me like Menno Harvey or trick me into sitting on his lap like Uncle Abe. He would never try and sneak into my room in the middle of the night. So, for those reasons, I liked him. I liked anyone who left me alone.

X
January 2018

*A*fter Rochelle returns to school, I retreat to the attic almost every day, sometimes just to sit in the square of sunlight and have a moment to myself. Titus and I have spent a decade building a successful business, but it often takes him away for several days at a time. I'm incredibly grateful that DJ and Darrel have become so helpful with their brother. They come in after school and play video games together, the kind that Dusty likes, so I can continue to write in my journal. I'm writing my story. Or should I say, I'm rewriting my story? So many others had written it for me and gotten it wrong. All these years later, people still point to me as an example of a bad Amish girl—the kind who tempts a married preacher, runs away, and gleefully lives in sin. Just like her mother, they say. But I'm nothing like her. I had four children with one husband; Mem had five children with three different men. I've never spent more than a few days away from my special needs son. My children are happy, kind and generous.

I remember this feeling of holding my pen mid-air, afraid to write the truth. I've done it before. The summer I turned fourteen, Mem gave me a diary, a small book of lined pages with a red leather cover and a gold lock. "You're a young woman now, and you need to record your daily activities," she'd said. "And remember, the *Gut Mun* is reading it, too." I'd wanted to write down my dreams and secrets. I remember as I held a pen over the first page, I thought some "dreams and secrets" would be fun to have. But Mem's warning interrupted my thoughts, and instead, I'd jotted down my chores for the day.

Standing in the attic with my new journal in my hands, I realize that if Mem's diary was in Datt's belongings, maybe mine is too. I find it several minutes after I start looking. It's been there all along, tucked away in the attic. Like Mem, I noted the weather, chores, and visitors. Like Mem, I left few suggestions as to how I actually felt. But I did leave myself one important clue. Six weeks into the diary, the winter after I turned fourteen, I'd started to write something, then scribbled it out, then scribbled over it again in different ink. I circled the date of the diary entry in a red ink pen. The red circle makes it all come rushing back to me. There were 26 red circles in my diary that year.

XI
July 1988

i was thrilled to turn fourteen, finally! I'd finished eighth grade, which meant no more school and no more Bertha. But I was also aware it was the end of my education, and I was supposed to forget about high school or college. I hated being a *maude*, but I accepted it as my fate and tried not to think about it. Instead, I tried to focus on the new little freedoms I did have. Outside of church, I could now wear a white, pleated *kapp* instead of a plain, black *kapp*, and now everyone would know I was a young woman, not a little girl. At home, I took over many of Mem's chores. But as I sewed yet another new set of blue curtains, I looked out the window at the passing cars and thought, "Someday I will drive one of those cars, and I will blast the radio as loud as it will go."

A few days later, Mem announced my fate. "Go pack a few sets of clothes and overnight things. You're going to go be Aden and Cevilla's *maude*."

"Cevilla?" I asked. "Our old *maude*?"

Mem nodded. "I'm taking you over in the horse and buggy this afternoon."

I had no time to say goodbye to Royal. Mem rushed me through chores, and before I knew it, we were in the buggy, driving up the road to my new home. Mem was unusually talkative. "You know Cevilla. She would come and stay with you before she was married. Her husband had a medical procedure and can't lift anything heavy."

"What kind of medical procedure?" I asked.

"Oh, nothing for you to know," she said with a smile.

When we pulled up to their trailer house, I tied the horse to the hitching pole and followed Mem inside. Cevilla stood over a small stove, cooking supper with one hand and holding a baby with the other. I stood near the door holding my suitcase with both hands and concentrated on a tear in the wallpaper above her head until she dropped the baby, named Elsie, into my arms. Baby Elsie smiled at me, and I found myself smiling back. I realized that I was rocking her back and forth after Mem handed me a bottle of warm milk.

"I remember she can be slow," Cevilla said to Mem, looking me over.

"Just tell her she can't eat 'til chores are done, and she'll hurry up," Mem answered. Cevilla laughed, and I pretended not to hear them. The door opened again, and her husband came into the house for supper. I saw a faint smile cross Mem's lips before she looked away and smoothed her hair around the edges of her kapp. Cevilla kept her eye on the oven. Mem asked if I remembered Cevilla's husband, Aden. I looked at him and was surprised to find him looking closely back at me. Embarrassed, I turned my attention back to the baby. Had Mem noticed? I'd always thought Aden was friendly, but the way Mem looked at him and he at me felt inappropriate. He nodded and said, "*Ve bish* (how are you)?" Then he washed his hands and sat down at the table. He seemed very polite. Perhaps I'd misjudged him.

The three older children ran into the room and piled onto their father's lap. Two-year-old Naomi tugged on his beard while he tickled one-year-old Delilah under her arms. Hermie, the oldest child, bounded up and down between them. I remained standing in the middle of the kitchen, lost in the comfort of rocking Elsie. Mem abruptly clasped her hands together and strode toward the door. "I need to get on home before it's dark." She looked at me from the open doorway. "Now do what they tell you to do, and do it right." Her eyes shifted to Cevilla, and they exchanged smiles. Then she was gone, and all I could hear was the faint clip-clop of Rex on the road as he hauled Mem back the way they came.

Cevilla brought a pan of apple crisp out of the oven. I'd never heard of anyone serving sweet apple crisp for supper, but the children all scrambled into their chairs before the dish hit the table.

"Lizzy!" Aden called out. "Come join us."

I hesitated, not wanting to let go of the baby, not ready to sit at the table with my new family. Mem thought I was a disappointment, and I wondered if they would, too.

"Put Elsie in her crib in our room back there," Cevilla said, sternly. "She'll be asleep soon enough."

I took my time, waiting for Elsie's eyes to flutter closed before I laid her in the crib. The children sat quietly eating, speaking only when spoken to, as good Amish children are supposed to. "Compared to my brothers and cousins, Aden and Cevilla's children behave like angels," I thought.

Each night after dinner, Cevilla took over with the kids while I went out to the barn to help Aden finish milking the cows. For the first few months, he said little besides instructing me how to work the equipment. The *Ordnung* forbid Amish from using power equipment, but since he worked as a manager at an English farm, he had gotten electric milkers to use on his own farm.

As summer gave way to autumn, the small farm came alive with loons wailing their way west. Green canopies covering the hills turned red and gold. Aden loved listening to rock music on the radio. Like Uncle Abe, he called it the Mallard Duck. I must have looked surprised because he chuckled and said, "I know listening to the radio is forbidden, but sinning in the barn is better than sinning in the home." The lyrics coming from the Mallard Duck were foreign to me, but I loved this new, exciting music that came pouring through the speakers. Aden would stop what he was doing and tilt his head to the side. "Listen to this part," he'd say. "I love this line." He'd sing along to make sure I understood.

Even indulging in eye contact with Aden began to feel like a sin. Eventually, I eased into his jokes and even laughed at a few, covering my mouth so as not to appear immodest. "Don't cover your smile," he said. "You have such a beautiful smile, such pretty full lips." He put his hand on my shoulder. At first, I wanted to pull away. I never saw affection between him and Cevilla, my parents, or any Amish couple. I didn't want to upset him or make him feel like he was doing something wrong. If I went along, maybe it would seem more natural. That's what I told myself.

By February, all color had disappeared from the landscape. Snow covered the spruce and red oak trees. The creeks froze and sparkled beneath the stars. The wind whipped through the cracks beneath the doors and rattled the windows. My fingers began to numb as I finished wiping off the teats of each cow. Cevilla and the children were in the house. I could see smoke coming from the chimney, blowing gray puffs into the empty sky. I worked a little faster, eager to finish so I could bring my stiff fingers back to life by the wood stove. The radio was louder that evening. I knew the song by heart and recited the words in my head. As I released the last milker from the cow, I felt Aden's hand nudge my shoulder. I jumped. He held a bottle of Schnapps in each hand. I wondered if he planned to drink them both. He held out a bottle, and I looked at the label: root beer flavor. Mem made homemade root beer soda pop at home, and root beer was my favorite flavor.

"There's a bad flu cold going around," he said. "This will help."

I hesitated until he nodded for me to accept it. I did, then held the bottle in my lap until he reached over to untwist the cap and place it in my sweaty palms. I took a short swallow, my first taste of alcohol, shuddering at the harsh, bitter flavor—so similar yet so different from the nonalcoholic root beer I'd had at home. He dragged a pail close to me and sat down. I could feel his breath on my neck, wicking away the bitter draft in the barn. Without turning my head, I could feel his eyes watching me. Feeling uncertain, I took another small sip. Then another. The Schnapps warmed my insides and lifted my mood.

"Why are you smiling?" he asked.

I covered my mouth. Datt's frowning face appeared in my mind, and I found myself staring at the cows, trying not to smile.

Aden laughed. "Drink up," he said.

I took a large swallow and coughed. Aden patted me on the back. When I regained my composure, his hand became still. For a moment, I thought the back of my dress might catch fire. I wondered how his hands could be so warm in such a cold place. Suddenly he looked serious as if he had something important to tell me.

"Follow me," he said and walked toward the barn doors. I stood and wiped my hands on my apron, hoping everything was okay. He stopped and turned out the lights, then remained still, his shadow looming across the floor. I paused and fumbled to put on my gloves. In a flash, I felt his hand reach around my waist, and the cold stone wall against my back. Before I could yell out, he stuck his wet tongue into my mouth and circled it around and around. He reached under my dress.

I was trapped. "It's okay," I tried to reassure myself. "It will be just like Uncle Abe. It will be over with quickly."

But no. As my back hit the wall, I felt a jagged edge of stone against my spine. I opened my mouth to scream, but the only thing that came out was a soft, "No." He bit down hard on my lip, and I clenched my eyes against the pain. "Who would hear me anyway?" I thought. The cold wall hit my spine again and again. "I have to obey him," I thought. "I have to do as I'm told."

"Relax, and it won't hurt so much," he whispered. "Just relax and enjoy it."

"He's mixing a batch," I realized. That's what they called this forbidden act. As his body moved, I tried to detach from everything he was doing, and I prayed for the mixing to be over.

Aden finally let go, and I stepped away. "Go down to the house now," he said. "Don't say a word to my wife or anyone, understand? I'll be home soon." I straightened my dress and walked away from the barn. The wind was blowing bitter cold. A perfect slice of quarter moon hung in the clear night sky. I looked up, wondering if God had seen what Aden did, wondering how He would punish my family. Would He burn our house down, too? Would He take Royal? But no *Gut Mun* looked down at me, and it was too cold to wait there for answers.

I stopped inside the outhouse and crouched down in the corner with my legs folded tight against my chest. It hurt so much inside. I rubbed the blood on my underwear with newspaper from the pile next to the bucket. Finally, I began to cry. From the deep pit of my stomach, tears welled up, bursting up through my shuddering ribcage and releasing into my apron, where I buried my head. "Why, why, why did I let things get to this point?" I asked myself over and over. "Now it's too late. I'm damaged goods. I should have fought back harder. I hate myself. I just want to die." I thought about praying, but I was crying too hard and didn't want Cevilla to hear me. "Is this His plan for me?" I wondered. "What did I do to make *Gut Mun* so angry?"

When I got back to the house, Cevilla and the children were in bed. I felt grateful for the small blessing of being able to avoid them. I went upstairs to my room, where the voices in my head continued. "I'm dirty, used. I'll never get married. No one will ever love me, and I can't even love myself. Who would want me?" I thought. "No one."

I listened to Aden walk into the house and place his boots by the wood stove to dry. I heard the door squeak open, the thud of wood chunks, and the bristle of a renewed flame. I listened to his footsteps cross the living room, the closing door, and the creak as he settled into bed with his wife. I buried my head into the pillow and cried until I fell asleep.

The next morning at breakfast, I tried not to make eye contact with Aden, but he acted like nothing happened, talking about the weather, as usual. I looked away from Cevilla, refusing to meet her eyes. I stayed busy with the children and felt guilty around them, too. What would they think of me if they ever knew? What would they think of their father? I felt sorry for them. I wondered if I'd ruined everything. But avoiding the barn or Aden was not an option. That afternoon, I kept looking over my shoulder with a heightened awareness that he would eventually come to the barn—nervous he might try and mix a batch with me again. I still hurt from the night before. The barn door opened. I braced myself.

"How's my Lizzy?" His voice sounded gentle and sincere. His tone was innocent of last night's wrongdoing. I turned off the milker and waited, tense. I didn't want to feel that pain again. "Sit down and take a break," he said. "You work too hard."

Relieved, I sat on the pail he'd set out next to him. "Am I in trouble?" I wondered. "Will he punish me for making him sin?"

He clicked on the radio and stayed quiet for a while. I tried to concentrate on the words of the song. "What is he waiting for?" I thought. I wasn't sure what to do, so I rubbed at an invisible stain on my apron. "Don't worry. I won't get you pregnant. Cevilla got me fixed."

I was speechless hearing that, so I just nodded. There was an awkward silence. "I bet you didn't know you're my favorite *maude*," he added.

"No," I whispered. I had never been anyone's favorite anything. "Why?" I wanted to ask.

He seemed to read my mind. "I like you. You're a special girl."

I continued scratching the imaginary spot on my apron. No one had ever called me special before. He gently laid his warm hand over my cold one, and I felt the heat of his skin soak into my fingers. When I finally mustered the courage to look at him, he seemed to be searching for words. He looked shy and nervous, nothing at all like the man who'd pinned me to the wall. Our eyes met and he continued. "*Gut Mun* isn't angry with us. Your Datt mixed with a *maude*, too. It's just the way it is sometimes." I stifled my shock and disbelief. Datt with a *maude*? Datt hurting anyone? Was Cevilla the *maude*? It couldn't be true. "And your Mem, well, let's just say you're not really Little Levi's daughter." In my heart, I'd always thought so, but it still hurt to hear it said out loud for the first time. Aden was especially kind to me for the rest of the week, and I wondered if he was sorry for what he'd done.

That weekend, he asked me to help him in the feed room again. As I lifted the corner of a large bag, he pushed me, and I fell backward onto the pile. Bits of grain swirled up and dried inside my throat. He was gentler this time, and it hurt less.

* * * * *

By early springtime, I began to do as Aden requested and relax. He asked me what I thought about songs on the Mallard Duck. He asked me how my day was going. He seemed to care.

Some days, it was as if the mixing never happened at all. One day, Aden snapped at me and Cevilla ignored me altogether. While Cevilla ate lunch with the children, I jumped in the buggy and rode the six miles back home where I walked straight past Mem and my siblings and upstairs to bed. Mem must have sent Royal upstairs to check on me. "What's wrong with you?" Royal asked. "Mem says to come downstairs."

I refused to budge. "Tell Mem I'm getting the flu and staying in bed today."

Something inside me had changed. I dreaded going back. Every day, I wore an obedient smile, but inside I was weeping. I had begun to have regular nightmares of being chased through the cornfields by a dark shadow whose identity was unknown to me. I considered telling Mem, Royal, or an English friend.

I thought I might have a chance the day Mem, Royal, and I went to an English funeral together. But I wasn't expecting to share a carriage with Aden. The buggy seat was only wide enough for two adults, and Royal sat on Mem's lap, leaving me no choice but to sit on top of Aden. Mem said nothing about it as I awkwardly tried to balance on his knee, avoiding the soft middle of his lap while waiting for Mem to stop the whole thing. Surely, she would think it inappropriate for me to sit on this grown man's lap. The soft part of Aden's lap didn't stay soft, however, and I bit my tongue all the way to the funeral and all the way back home.

I tried to pull myself out of my funk. It couldn't be as bad as I thought, I told myself. He must love me a lot to commit such a sin. I struggled to piece together all the conflicting beliefs and experiences, and I even began to look forward to a fishing trip he'd promised me. I told myself it would be a chance to get away from the house and chores and Cevilla. "I take every *maude* fishing as a thank you," he said.

The next morning, after chores and a quick breakfast, we headed for the creek. I sat with my hands folded in my lap, watching the scenery. The fishing poles rattled on top of the buggy, and the horse slowed as the road became steep and narrow. Aden jerked the reins before the last turn toward the Root River, and his horse obediently stepped off the road and into a thicket. "Shall we see what lies off the beaten path?" Aden asked.

We were barely off the main road before he was hitching the horse to a tree and had his hands all over me. The hard, wooden buggy seat banged against my spine. "Relax," Aden said. "Relax and enjoy it."

When it finally ended, he grabbed a bottle of Schnapps and took a long swig before handing it to me. I took the bottle, tipping it to my mouth and letting the liquor drip slowly down my throat, hoping it would numb the rest of my body. Eventually, the warm fuzzy feeling overcame the pain in my back, and we headed to the fishing hole. As Aden fed the horse, a sudden thunderstorm drove me back into the buggy. I hid behind the curtain that separated the back seat, laughing as Aden came tumbling in beside me.

The sky rumbled and cracked, and he wrapped his arms around my shoulders. Lightning ricocheted, startling the horse. I'd never been held this way. This time, when he kissed me, it felt different from the mixing. I felt safe and loved, like nothing bad could happen. I wanted to feel this way forever. Part of me wanted him to leave Cevilla and his children and run away with me. But I knew Mem, Datt, Mummy, and Doddie—and especially *Gut Mun*—would never let that happen. "He will punish you," I thought. "Just like he punished the Borntragers."

"Rain stopped." Aden hopped out of the buggy, set up the fishing rods, and tossed the lines into the creek. I quickly fell asleep from the Schnapps, waking an hour later when a fish thudded into the bucket beside me. Aden laughed. "I'll tell everyone you caught that one, so they won't know you were passed out all day." He leaned over and splashed water onto my face. "You'd better sober up on the way back home."

I looked around. "Home?"

"We're already late for chores."

"Chores," I thought and sighed. The last thing I wanted to think about was work. I wasn't even bothered when Aden mixed a batch again before heading home. As we turned onto the main road, he pointed past me into the bushes and slowed the horse. A small plastic rectangle with dark thread looped through two holes lay on the gravel. "See what it is!" Aden called out. I picked it up and handed it to him.

"What is it?" I asked.

"A cassette tape." He read the label. "Fleetwood Mac."

"What a strange name," I said. "When can we listen to it?"

He winked. "Can you keep another secret?"

I looked at him sideways, like I'd seen Mem do when she teased Datt. "What do you think?"

"I got you a Walkman." He reached under the seat and handed me a small black box with headphones. "When you listen to it, think of me." He dropped me off in front of the barn, and I did the evening milking listening to Fleetwood Mac and thinking about Aden and me.

I waited for the next fishing trip, the next thunderstorm, the next time he would put his arms around me and make me feel safe. But Aden went back to business as usual. Some days, he turned on the Mallard Duck and pushed me into the hayloft. Other days, he barely spoke to me, and I was just a *maude* again, no one special. A few weeks after the fishing trip, I told Mem that I was done working for Aden and Cevilla. I expected her to argue and planned to stand my ground. But Mem just said, "Okay," and went back to her housework. I wondered what was wrong with her. Why wasn't she forcing me to go back? Part of me missed Aden as soon as she said it, but I hated the looks I was getting at *Gma* and the whispers behind my back. "She is a *schlud* (slut) and a *hoodah* (whore)." I had no idea how they knew.

XII
June 1990

O ne morning after I'd returned home, Mem hollered up the steps for Royal and me to get up early. "Lizzy! Royal!" We came downstairs, rubbing the sleep from our eyes. Mem sat at the table, eating cinnamon rolls just out of the oven. "Go do chores quickly, and then wash up and put clean clothes on. We are going to the clinic in Decorah today."

Royal and I looked at each other, puzzled. "We're both feeling fine," I said. "We aren't sick."

Mem waved me away. "It's just a routine checkup at a clinic. I'll tell you more, later."

We quickly finished our chores and made lunch for Datt and our brothers, since we were getting back in the late afternoon. Henry hitched Rex to the buggy and drove us to Canton, where we caught the bus to Decorah. Once on the bus, we pressed Mem for answers. She finally gave in. "You're going to get some pills to help with your heavy periods. Now be quiet, or I'll tell Datt about your Walkmans."

Wide-eyed, Royal and I looked at each other. I liked having the monthly excuse to get out of chores even though I had some minor cramps and discomfort during my period, but Royal had bad cramping and distress during her period. "It sure would be nice if we didn't have to have the *bes en cluck* (menstrual cycle)," Royal said. I listened as she chatted away, secretly wondering if what Mem said was true. I'd once heard Cevilla and Mem arguing over "the pill." Cevilla said she took it to ease her period cramps. Mem said those pills also stopped a woman from getting pregnant, and it was just an excuse to mix a batch without having to watch the bread rise. I wondered, did this mean Mem knew what Aden had done to me? And if so, is that why she brought Royal, only fourteen years old and still painfully innocent? She wouldn't be for long if Aden or Mem had any influence. A sickening thought ricocheted through me: What if they sent Royal to be Aden and Cevilla's *maude* in my place?

We walked into the clinic, where I tried to ignore the glares coming from the English people in the waiting room. Mem went to talk to a lady at the desk, and then a nurse came and took Royal and me to separate rooms in the back. Once inside the exam room, the nurse handed me a thin paper apron and told me to take everything off. "Those, too," she said, pointing at my bloomers. Then she returned with the doctor, who told me to spread my legs and put my feet into metal brackets on either side of the table. He swung a lamp around so that it hovered over me, then clicked on the light. I stayed quiet, hardly breathing. I just looked straight up at the ceiling while he stuck something cold inside me. I thought it must be some kind of clamp like Datt had in his shop to hold wood together. I thought about my sister. Where was she? Was this happening to her, too?

Finally, the nurse said that they were done and would leave the room so I could get dressed. I put my clothes back on, suddenly grateful for each layer, wondering what just happened. Back in the waiting room, Royal and I sat together as Mem paid the bill. Royal was trying hard not to cry. "It was terrible," she whispered. "They stuck something up my pee pee, and it hurt so bad." I forgot about my lingering cramps and wondered what they had done to her. At least for me, it didn't hurt.

Mem was silent about it until later that evening as Royal and I were getting ready for bed. She came upstairs with two round compacts of pills. We were to take one each day at the same time. "Don't tell anyone about the clinic or the pills," she added. "If Datt asks, just say we went to look at fabric, but came home empty-handed." We nodded.

Before leaving the room, Mem turned to me and whispered, "Don't forget what I said. Every day." So, I took a pill every day until they ran out thirty days later. Mem never mentioned it again.

* * * * *

A few weeks later, Royal also went away to work as a *maude*. Usually, I craved the extra bed space, but I missed her. One night, I knelt at the top of the stairs listening to Mem and Datt whispering in the kitchen. They spoke quietly, as if they knew I was there. Mem had worked me harder than usual that day, and eventually, I crept back into bed and fell asleep.

In the middle of the night, Mem shook me awake. "Come downstairs," she said. I obeyed and followed her to the kitchen where Datt, Aden, and Cevilla sat around the table. Empty beer cans had been pushed aside to make room for a card game. I could smell the alcohol from across the room. I walked closer and stood a few feet away, waiting. Cevilla shuffled the deck again and again, the cards blurring in her hands. The cards snapped still as she looked at me. "You know you were asking for it. Everyone knows it's your fault. You're to stay away from my husband."

I hesitated, waiting for Mem and Datt to defend me. Surely, they knew I was a good girl. But neither would meet my eyes. They just stared down at the cards in Cevilla's hands, as if waiting for her to deal the next round. Shame rose in my chest. I pushed it down, determined not to cry. It was all my fault and now he was done with me. No man would ever want me as his wife. I desperately wanted someone to glance up at me and give me a sign that it wasn't my fault. But they never looked up. They kept looking at Cevilla. "You can go now," Mem announced.

I ran back to my room and started quietly packing. I would run away from home and disappear. Or I'd kill myself. I had no idea where I was going or how I would end things, but I couldn't bear the thought of being trapped with my parents while everyone I knew stared and whispered behind my back. I felt humiliated on a daily basis. I was no longer Lizzy. I was a home-wrecker and a whore, an embarrassment. I had watched life go by from behind the blue curtains that kept me hidden from the world, longing to be a part of it. But I was now resigned that I deserved no such thing; I did not deserve the world. It was time for me to disappear. I took the last few minutes to paint my nails bright pink with a bottle of polish I'd been hiding. I tiptoed down the stairs, carrying my shoes so as not to make a sound. But when I got to the bottom, Mem and Datt were waiting for me.

"Where are you going?" Datt asked.

"I'm running away," I answered. I wouldn't let them stop me.

"Where to?"

"Anywhere, but here."

"Turn around and go back to your room," Datt said.

I knew he wouldn't let me go, and there was nothing to do but wait for another chance.

They followed me up the stairs to my room, standing in the doorway.

"Running away will just make things worse," Mem added. "No one will give you a home anyway because of your bad attitude and sinful nature." I stopped listening and focused on scratching the polish off my nails. "Someone saw you!" Mem said suddenly. "A neighbor who walked into the barn to use the phone seen you two." My heart froze inside my chest. Someone had seen Aden and me? Mem continued. "The English who own that farm know what's going on and so do a bunch of the Amish. You really did it this time." Datt looked down at the floorboards and said nothing.

I'd barely fallen asleep when Mom shook me awake a second time. Moonlight spilled over the empty spot next to me where Royal should've been. I sat up.

"What is it?" I asked, rubbing my eyes, annoyed that I'd woken up in my bed and not far away as I'd hoped.

Mem shoved an empty banana box into my lap. "Pack up this box and get dressed."

I rubbed my eyes. "Where are we going?"

"Just do it and be quiet, so you don't wake your Datt." She walked silently back downstairs.

I changed out of my nightgown, wondering if I'd been called to help with a new baby. I opened the box and reached for my Bible on the dresser, as Mem would expect me to pack it. But instead, I pulled my favorite Danielle Steele novel from under the mattress and hid the Bible in its place. I slipped my Walkman in my pocket. Downstairs, Mem handed me half a loaf of bread and an avocado, which I added to the box as I waited for an explanation. "Did someone have a baby?" I whispered. Mem put her finger to her lips and hurried me out the back door. The wind whipped briskly for a summer's night, and I noticed the buggy wasn't hitched. Mem handed me a flashlight. "I can't deal with all this drama you've caused. You're making us all miserable. You have to go for a while, at least until people stop talking."

"Where will I go?" I asked.

"Darlene said she'll look after you for a bit. Walk to the abandoned house up the road there, and she'll pick you up in the morning." Darlene was an English woman I'd helped with housekeeping.

"But you and Datt told me to stay."

"That's the last thing anyone really wants."

I stood there for a moment, trying to think of something else to say. Suddenly, I felt like I didn't really want to go, not like this, not with Mem kicking me out in the middle of the night. I shivered, unsure if it was because of the chill or the long, pitch-black road in front of me. Mem crossed her arms and jerked her chin toward the road, motioning for me to go. I took a few steps. All I heard was the soft brushing of tall grass against my ankles. When I looked back, Mem was gone.

I felt utterly alone. Suddenly, I had to face the realization that running away on my own terms would have simply ended in my turning around and going back up to bed. The decision to stay would have been a small freedom in itself. For a moment, I was sure Mem was just trying to scare me. Surely, the thought of being swallowed up by the dark unknown was punishment enough. I longed to hear the squeal of the back door open and Mem's sharp voice breaking the silence, calling me back inside. I would take a hundred whacks with a sewing belt; I would even apologize to Aden and Cevilla, if she would open the door and call my name. Only the wind answered, howling into the dark road ahead. I felt numb with fear. I started walking.

* * * * *

The abandoned house was only about half a mile away, but it might as well have been a hundred. The dark stretched endlessly in front of me, blurring the lines of the road and the sky and whatever was in between that was invisible to me. I'd never been out walking alone late at night. I was too scared to turn on the flashlight in case someone or something saw me from the woods. Every sound made me twitch and wonder if some creature was crawling toward me, or worse, a person, a man. Aden. I shivered at the thought of him, then pushed him away, trying to think of something comforting. Royal. I wanted to pretend she was walking beside me. I might not be so scared then. But the warm feeling iced over at the thought of Mem telling her I'd run away. She'd think I'd abandoned her. I was truly alone now. Not even the distant light of a farmhouse broke the flat landscape. The sky looked back at me, dull and empty.

The house finally appeared, looming in jagged shadows off the road. A sliver of moon peeked from behind a heavy curtain of clouds and glinted against the broken windows. The screen door hung from its hinges, and someone had spray-painted an ugly word beside it. I stopped, unable to walk any closer. Instead, I walked around the back and clicked on the flashlight, hoping there might be a safer place to sleep. Empty cans and trash were strewn across the back porch. A small shadow flitted from one discarded item to the next. The light from my flashlight rested on something yellow, and I could tell it was a blanket. I crept toward it before snatching it away and running from the house.

I smoothed the blanket over a flat patch of tall grass and lay on one half, pulling the other half over me, but it was hard to get warm. Every time I closed my eyes, I felt something crawling on my bare skin or tickling my ear. A branch snapped in the distance. I froze, unsure if I should run or try and sink further into the ground. I prayed it was only a deer or even a coyote. I could almost see Datt's grim face stomping through the cornfield to drag me back to Mem. Or perhaps Aden would find me first. Which would be worse?

I slipped on my headphones and pressed play on my Walkman. Cher's rich voice drowned out the frightening silence and helped me forget where I was. As much as I wanted to think about something else, I saw Aden's face. I hated what he'd done to me. I hated everyone whispering behind my back mocking and blaming me for causing him to sin. The tears I'd been holding back rushed forward. At first, I felt nothing, just wetness spreading over my cheeks. I almost welcomed their warmth until they seemed unstoppable, and I was sure I'd soon drown in a puddle. I stopped caring. I wanted the ground to swallow me up.

I woke up to the familiar sound of Datt's sawmill grinding in the distance, then rolled over and tucked my face back under the blanket. Dew sprinkled my nose and hair. I sat up to shake it off and squinted against the bright sun. I looked toward the sawmill. By now, Datt must be thinking I'd run away, but his life went on. He didn't come to look for me, or if he had, he did a bad job of it. My stomach grumbled. I opened the banana box and ate half of my sandwich, planning to save the other half for later. But I was still hungry, and Mem said Darlene would come first thing in the morning. I ate the other half and opened my book. But an hour passed by, and there was no sign of Darlene.

The sun hovered at well past noon when I heard a horse clopping and the crunch of a buggy turning into the driveway. I propped myself up and peered cautiously over the tips of the grass, staying hidden. It was Mem. She hitched the horse to a tree. As she walked toward the back of the house, she shaded her eyes with her hand. She looked alarmed at the condition of the porch and stopped short of walking up the steps to the door. She gazed out toward the field, as if she knew I was there. I ducked down, not ready to see her, fighting the pangs of hunger stabbing at my stomach. Let her think I'd been dragged off by a maniac, I thought, maybe then she'd feel bad. But I knew Mem too well. She might be relieved instead, and I certainly didn't want that.

As Mem walked back to the buggy, I stood up and stomped after her, furious she would give up so quickly. I left the dirt on my *kapp* and the grass stains on my dress. Let her see how I'd suffered! But Mem refused to turn around until I stood right behind her, demanding her attention. She took her time rummaging through the buggy before pulling out another sandwich, some fruit, and a small jar of milk. "I was in Canton," she said finally, "so I thought I'd bring you some food. Darlene will be here this afternoon when her daycare lets out." She handed me the food and heaved herself back onto the buggy seat. Rex raised his head and huffed into my shoulder. I felt grateful for his brief acknowledgment and rested my hand on his nose. Mem jerked the reins. Then she and Rex were gone.

The sun sat low in the sky when Darlene finally pulled up in a red van and stood beside it, assessing me. "Is that all you brought with you?" She asked, eyeing the box, which now held only my book. I nodded. She sighed, got back in the car, and leaned over to unlock the passenger door. Little things seemed to annoy her tremendously on the drive back to her house, and she complained about it all: the route was too slow, she'd come out of her way, the blinker stayed on too long. I felt like an inconvenience. Even so, I was thrilled to get English clothing at a garage sale the next day. And a few days later, Darlene's daughter gave me a perm in their kitchen! I tried to show my gratitude by keeping her house spotless, which was the reason I was there, but I could tell that Darlene was unhappy with me. After a week, she said I needed to find another situation. Mem told me that she wasn't surprised that yet another person couldn't handle me, and I'd have to go to my Aunt Melissa's in Battle Creek, Michigan.

Darlene bought me a ticket to Battle Creek. Early the next morning, she dropped me off at the Greyhound station. I waited on my own in the dim early morning light. The station was still closed when the bus arrived. My book and new English clothes sat on the seat beside me in an old suitcase Darlene gave me.

When the bus arrived in Battle Creek, I got off and walked to a nearby shopping center where a Kmart, bank, gas station, and diner stood locked and empty. I found a payphone and called Aunt Melissa's number, as Mem instructed, but there was no answer. As the businesses opened, I took turns at each one, casually trying to hang around in the waiting areas. But I kept getting kicked out. For several hours, a man in a pick-up truck circled the parking lot watching me. I called my aunt's house over and over again, pretending I was talking on the unanswered line.

My stomach sank as the sun dipped below the horizon. The pick-up truck had disappeared, but I had no money and hadn't eaten. Eventually, a woman working at the gas station invited me inside to use the phone behind the counter, and Aunt Melissa finally picked up. "I'm so tired," she said, "but I'll drive the two hours to pick you up, since I said I would."

As I handed the phone back to the station attendant, she looked me over and sighed. "I seen you standing outside most of the day. Have you eaten anything?" I shook my head. "My name is Sheila, what's yours?"

"Elizabeth," I said. She slid a bag of peanuts across to me and picked up the phone again. "I'm calling my husband, Chuck, to take you to get something to eat." She must have seen my face tense up because she told me to relax. I cringed at the word. *Relax.* Aden's word. "Don't worry," she said. "I trust him."

My hunger trumped any concerns about her husband. He picked me up in a truck and drove me across the parking lot to the diner, talking about his back problems while I wolfed down a burger. But then, back in his truck, he wanted to talk more. He wouldn't start the engine. He just leaned out the open window, smoking, and asking personal questions. I offered to walk back to the gas station. He reached over, grabbed my hand, and put it on his thigh, and when I tried to flick it away, he grabbed my hand harder and put it on his crotch.

"No!" I shouted and jumped so hard my back thudded against the door.

"Alright, alright, calm down," he said. I'd never seen that look on a man's face before: startled and amused at the same time. "Gee, you're a feisty little one, aren't you?" His shoulders eased as he seemed to consider me in a new light. His eyes slowly assessed this new me, pausing on the top buttons of my blouse and jeans. He chuckled, as if I'd told him a secret. The sound trickled along my spine making me shudder. "Don't worry, farm girl. It's all good. I like you." He started the engine, grinning as I remained crumpled in the corner, ready to spring as soon as the door opened.

As he pulled away from the diner, I realized my knuckles had turned white, still curled around the door handle. The truck picked up speed.

"Aren't you taking me back to the gas station?" Chuck had driven out of the shopping center parking lot and back toward the highway.

"I want someone to meet you," he said. "It'll just take a minute."

"My aunt is gonna be waiting for me."

"Your aunt ain't coming anytime soon, and Sheila ain't the maternal type." Chuck leaned over and lowered his voice to a whisper. "We're gonna have some fun." I squinted my eyes and tightened my lips, trying my best to look menacing. But Chuck just said, "Aw, farm girl, you're cute when you squish your nose up like that."

He pulled into the driveway of a small, ramshackle house on a cement lot broken by zigzags of dead, yellow grass. A man walked out of the open garage; his hands tucked into his jeans pocket. "This is Kevin," Chuck said.

A trucker cap pulled over Kevin's brow cast a deep shadow, so that his eyes were hard to see. He ambled up to the passenger side window and looked me over, the way Datt looked at horses for auction. Kevin shrugged. "She's okay. Nothing special."

Chuck grabbed my thigh and squeezed. "Look at that. That's milk fat. Fresh off the farm."

"Is she a virgin?" Kevin asked.

There was a pause, and they looked at me, as if waiting for an answer. Even if I was willing to answer the question, how would I answer? Of course, Aden had taken my virginity, but did it count if I had no choice? I wondered if I could still be a virgin in God's eyes. Chuck answered for me. "She might as well be. She's still under eighteen, so we'll get a good price."

"I'm not for sale," I stammered.

Chuck laughed, but Kevin glared back at me, unamused by my outburst. He moved closer and reached out to touch my face. The tips of his calloused fingers brushing against my skin felt like burning needles. I instinctively smacked his hand away. Enraged, Kevin grabbed me around the throat. "I'll trade you in for horse feed," he growled.

Chuck wrestled me out of Kevin's grip. "Easy, easy. She ain't gonna make no money if she's dead."

I was scared, but I could tell Kevin had reservations about me. I wanted to keep it that way to get out of this situation.

"My aunt is a very worried person. She'll send the police looking for me if I'm not waiting at the station."

"I thought you said she was a runaway," Kevin snapped.

Chuck grinned, as if he had just shot a prize buck and Kevin was admiring it. "Oh, she's a runaway alright. She just ain't quite ready to be plucked, but she'll be worth the wait."

Kevin seemed to lose interest. "I told you I don't need the cops up my ass. Don't bring me any more of these girls with pain-in-the-ass families. Bring her back to her aunt." He turned and went back inside. Chuck snapped his fingers at me. "Write down your aunt's number."

I stared back at him. "What for?"

"In case Kevin comes looking for you, I can make sure you're okay. You know I saved your life back there." Eager to get back to the gas station. I jotted it down, forgetting to come up with a fake number.

When we finally got back to the gas station, I wandered around the lot, keeping away from Chuck and Sheila. I was so relieved to see my aunt. I scrambled into the back seat. Aunt Melissa turned to look at me cowering behind her. Her friend in the front passenger seat didn't try to hide her horror at my appearance: the mismatched garage sale clothes, Darlene's daughter's first attempt at a perm, and my amateur attempts at applying eyeliner. I must have looked like quite a sight.

Melissa sighed heavily. "Lizzy, I'm disappointed in you. Did you say thank you to the nice lady and her husband?" Melissa tilted her head and gestured toward the gas station, where Chuck's truck was still parked and Sheila presumably still working inside.

I mumbled an indeterminate response.

She shook her head, disappointed, but started the car. "Teenagers," she muttered to her friend. "So ungrateful."

I'd pictured Aunt Melissa coming alone to meet me, the two of us riding side by side, bonding over our shared family history. I strained to hear their conversation, desperate to connect somehow and to make them like me. But I couldn't hear more than a few words over the din of the car radio. I felt utterly alone in the world, disgusted with Aunt Melissa, her stupid friend, Mem, Datt, Aden, everyone. I would prove to all of them that I was nothing like them. They could keep their world. The English world wasn't great either, certainly not if it was filled with people like Chuck and Kevin. Maybe I didn't belong anywhere.

When we got to the house, Melissa's husband, Raymond, watched with a concerned expression as his wife nervously flitted about the house setting me up in the guest room. He stared from beneath bushy, gray eyebrows as I gulped down a glass of milk at their kitchen table. Finally, he sat down across from me. His eyes looked kind from behind the thick lenses of his glasses. "Not getting along with your mother, huh?"

I shrugged, then shook my head. "Not really."

"Yeah, your mom and I were neighbors growing up, and I don't blame you one bit. Maybe that means you're okay."

I permitted him a faint smile and looked into the empty glass.

"You want some more?"

I nodded. He opened the fridge and refilled my glass, then put the carton to his lips and tipped back his head. I stared at him, wide-eyed. He chucked the empty carton across the room into the bin and put his finger to his lips. "Don't tell your aunt." I laughed then, for the first time since I could remember. Raymond dragged his chair closer to mine and looked back to make sure he could still hear Melissa making up the guest bed. I braced myself, waiting for him to whisper that he would see me later when he crawled into my bed. But Raymond just leaned in and said, "Your mother has issues."

I tilted my head in a way I hoped looked encouraging. He was the first person I'd ever heard say it that way, and I wanted to hear more. "What kind of issues?" I asked.

"Serious ones," Raymond said.

I was all ears. The phone rang, too loud and sharp for the late hour and the calm of the house. Raymond tensed. "Gee, it's late for a phone call."

Melissa came to the doorway with the cordless phone. "It's for you," she said, holding it just out of my reach. "Elizabeth," she added, dramatically.

My hand shook slightly as I took the receiver. "Hello?"

"Hey, farm girl."

I hung up. "Wrong number," I said.

Melissa crossed her arms and stared at me. "Why is a man calling you here?" she asked.

"I don't know," I lied. I wanted to explain, but it was too hard.

"You're lying!" Aunt Melissa turned to her husband. "She's just like her mother."

Raymond looked so disappointed.

I stayed seated, hoping he would go back to telling me what was wrong with Mem and let me know that I was nothing like her. But the moment was lost. I cleared my throat to say something, but nothing came out. After a pause, Raymond slid his chair away from the table and stood up, then dropped his hand on my shoulder before walking away.

I wanted to jump up and take it all back. I wanted to go back to sitting with Raymond, asking more questions about Mem. I wanted Aunt Melissa to see how different I was from Mem. But they had gone to bed.

If only I hadn't gone to the diner with Chuck. If only I had run from the car afterwards. If only I'd given him a fake phone number. It was so hard to get anything right. I was bad, just like Mem said. When Raymond and Aunt Melissa returned home from work the next day, they had made a decision.

"You can't stay here," Raymond said, "but we'll get you a ticket back home, and you can work things out with your mother."

"Please don't send me back," I pleaded. "It's not my fault he's calling."

"If you didn't want him to call, you wouldn't have given him your information," Aunt Melissa interrupted. "Your mother used to do the same thing. She'd get into trouble with some man, then come running here to hide from the consequences. I was hoping you'd be different." She crossed her arms and refused to look at me again.

Tears sprang to my eyes as I looked to Raymond, hoping he would see how good I was and let me stay. But he followed Melissa's lead.

A few days later, Raymond drove me to the bus station in silence. I was headed to LaCrosse. Instead of arranging for me to come back home, Mem had answered a newspaper ad requesting a babysitter in exchange for room and board. There was so much I wanted to say, but nothing came out. I stared out the car window to hide the tears streaming down my face. I leaned into the oncoming wind as it flicked them away. Raymond gave me some food and a $5 bill, and he stood outside the bus until it pulled away.

XIII
LaCrosse, WI
September 1990

When my bus arrived in LaCrosse, a woman with flaming red hair was waiting for me in a blue convertible. A wind-swept toddler sat in the back, looking alarmed. Cherry introduced her two-year-old daughter, Taylor, and told me to buckle up, we were going on an adventure. I almost got excited for a moment as I pictured the possibilities of Cherry and I cruising around in her convertible without a care in the world. Instead, we ended up at her broken-down house next to a dive bar. Once we were inside, we moved Taylor's crib out of the bedroom and into the living room next to the couch. Scooping up clothes and toys, Cherry told me to make myself comfortable. There were sheets in the hallway closet and leftovers in the fridge. She had a date, and she was eager to get out of the house for a few hours. Then she left for the night, leaving me with Taylor.

Thankfully, Taylor was used to watching TV for hours on end, and I took the opportunity to lay down on the couch and just be depressed. But Cherry soon made it clear how much she expected in exchange for the lumpy sofa and the cold cereal we ate three times a day. At the end of my first week, I found enough ingredients to bake a loaf of bread, which Taylor and I ate half of before Cherry returned from work. "Where'd you get that?" she asked, a slight look of panic crossing her face.

"I made it," I replied.

She eyed the bread suspiciously. "Out of what?"

"Flour, yeast, and salt."

Cherry tore off a piece and looked at it carefully before gingerly putting it in her mouth. "Can you bake a bunch more of these by tomorrow?"

"I'd need more ingredients," I said.

Chewing vigorously, she tore off a piece of newspaper and handed me a pen. "Write down what you need, and I'll go borrow it from the neighbors."

Cherry came back with bags of half-used flour, yeast, and a lot of other things I hadn't requested. "Use it all," she said. I baked a dozen loaves that night, which Cherry took with her the next day to the factory where she worked. She returned, having sold all the bread, with more ingredients and supplies in tow. Each night, after taking care of Taylor, preparing dinner and cleaning up, I baked bread. Before long, she had me making sweet rolls, cookies, and pies, all of which she sold at the factory. I never saw a dime, but Cherry said the extra money almost made up for the difference in her water bill, which she insisted had skyrocketed since I arrived.

One day before her shift started, Cherry brought me with her to the factory to deliver the orders. Cherry carried a tower of baked goods as I pushed Taylor in her stroller through the factory doors. As Cherry chatted with the receptionist, a tall man with a dark goatee and a bandanna wrapped around his head ambled into the office. "Hey, there, little lady," he drawled, his eyes drifting down my body. I felt a burst of energy explode like confetti in my chest, but I tried to act casual. "Hey," I said and looked down.

He sat on the edge of the table (he was too cool for a chair) dangerously near my legs. "Are you the famous baker who's making us all fat?" I nodded. He took the package from me and stood up, towering over me, but somehow still too close. I was frozen in place. A grin melted over his angular face. "You're cute," he said. "You ever been on a motorcycle?" I shook my head no, but smiled by accident. "What's your name?"

"Lizzy," I replied and flipped my hair the way I'd seen Cherry do a hundred times.

"I'm Maverick." He put the package on the desk and slung his arm over my shoulder.

Cherry rolled her eyes. "Uh oh, Maverick found his next victim." He waved her away and steered me toward the door. "Where are you going?" she asked.

Maverick held open the door for me like a princess. "We're running away together!"

"Okay," Cherry laughed. "She's got my kid, so bring her right back."

I tried to look cute as I walked past, but the wheel on Taylor's stroller got stuck and Maverick had to help me straighten it out in order to get Taylor through the door. I could smell the crisp leather of Maverick's jacket as he guided me across the parking lot toward a shiny black and chrome motorcycle. "You got the perfect backside for a motorcycle," he said.

I gasped. "Thank you," I said, unsure if that was the right answer.

"You wanna' go for a ride?"

I looked down at Taylor, who was cranky and ready for a nap. "Can we all fit?"

Maverick threw his head back and laughed. "That's a new one. But no, I'll pick you up tonight after Cherry gets off."

A night away from Cherry and Taylor! I was so happy. I raced back home with Taylor as if running would make the day go faster. Instead, time seemed to slow down. I spent the afternoon planning an elaborate excuse to tell Cherry, but as soon as she got home, she asked why I was still in my jeans and t-shirt. "Maverick is picking you up soon!" she yelled. "What are you wearing? You can't wear that!"

Cherry slid open her closet door and rifled through hangers packed so tightly she could barely move them. "Here," she said, handing me a pink blouse. "Try this on." As soon as I turned around to show her one outfit, Cherry was giving me another to try. It was the kind of thing I imagined Royal and I doing together if we had a closet full of clothes we could wear whenever we pleased. When Maverick showed up, I was wearing tight jeans and a leather jacket, trying not to bite off the hot pink gloss Cherry had carefully applied to my lips.

Outside, Maverick swung onto the bike and waited for me to climb on. It was hard to tell if the excited rumbling I felt was coming from me or the engine. There was no extra room on the seat, but Maverick insisted I could fit if I wrapped my arms around him and leaned into his back. The bike roared and jumped, and we shot out of the parking lot, leaving all my nerves behind. I was barely able to hold onto him tightly enough. We drove to a small bar at the edge of town. I'd never been inside a bar before nor had a drink besides Aden's root beer Schnapps. Right away, I felt tipsy. Maverick leaned in and kissed me, and everything around us disappeared. No one had kissed me since Aden, and this felt different, as if it would never end. I pulled away. There were people watching. "Maybe we should go," Maverick whispered in my ear.

Maverick kissed me again before we got on the bike, and once again in front of Cherry's house before he dropped me off. When I came in, she giggled and said, "I saw you making kissy-face with Maverick."

The next time Maverick came to the house, it was to see Cherry, and I had to babysit while they went on a date to the movies. My heart dropped. Maverick had seemed so sincere. But I was learning that lots of men who seemed sincere were not. I began looking in the paper for another job.

* * * * *

A few weeks later, a new family came to pick me up from Cherry's house, and I was relieved to go. Right away, Mindy and her husband, Brian, explained I'd mostly be working weekends and was free to attend the local high school during the week. I surged with excitement, then fear, at the thought of going back to school. Their three kids asked me lots of questions, but my mind was spinning with possibilities. Maybe I could have the kind of life I'd dreamed of after all. I pictured myself walking through the school hallways, my favorite books clutched to my chest, then at a big desk in my own office, talking to clients on the phone. For the first time, I could see it clearly. Someday, I would be free.

As soon as my first weekend with Brian and Mindy ended, I knew I wanted to stay. Mindy was only ten years older than me, and we took care of the house and kids together, more like sisters than employer and employee. We both loved *Twin Peaks* and *Days of Our Lives*. Brian was like the dads I'd read about in books. He was never angry or too busy for us. He drove us places and carried our things. He seemed genuinely interested in what each of us thought. Brian and Mindy took me to my first non-Amish church service and gave me my first English Bible. Finally, a Bible I could read on my own. Over time, I even became comfortable enough to tell them small snippets here and there about my life before I'd met them. I got a part-time job waiting tables. I was good at it and loved the customers, even the grumpy ones and those who didn't tip. I loved counting out my money at the end of the day, smoothing out each bill, and placing them in a neat pile, before rolling them up in a rubber band and hiding the wad in the lining of my purse, the way Mindy showed me.

On my first day of ninth grade, eating breakfast was impossible despite Brian's concern that it would affect my concentration. He wanted all his kids to do well, he said. As soon as we drove up to the giant brick building, I changed my mind about high school. Hundreds of people milled about the front lawn. I had never seen so many people my age together. Brian pulled on the parking brake and stretched his arm protectively behind me. "I know you come from a different world," he said. "This is ten times harder for you than anyone else. But you deserve this just as much, and I believe in you. Go get 'em, and I'll be here to pick you up afterward."

I got out of the car and followed the rows of shuffling shoes in front of me, not daring to look up in case I made eye contact with anyone. I sat frozen in class, too afraid to speak up.

Each night at Brian and Mindy's house, after we finished dinner and I helped put the kids to bed, Mindy insisted on doing the dishes so Brian could help me with homework. "You're good with numbers," he said one night when I brought home a perfect math test. Mindy agreed, adding that I should apply for college scholarships. "You've overcome so much, Lizzy."

I looked up at her. "I have?"

Mindy shut off the sink and came to sit beside us. "Sure, you have. I've never met anyone who started working at six years old."

"Or wasn't able to go to high school," Brian added.

"Who had no choice but to be a housewife and mother," Mindy continued.

"Who was taken advantage of."

"Raped."

Raped. It was the first time I'd heard anyone call what Aden and I had done as rape. I must've said it out loud because Mindy touched my hand. How could it be rape? I thought I loved Aden, maybe not at first, but as time went on it seemed like love.

Mindy lifted my chin. "That's not love, that's called grooming."

I thought about it for a moment, wondering if she was right. No one in my home ever talked about love. No one said they loved me until Aden said it in the barn. I had no idea what it meant.

She patted my hand, trying to keep me present. "Lizzy, I know they treated you like an adult, but you were, and still are, a child. Do you understand that?"

"I'm very mature for my age." I raised an eyebrow, a skill I'd practiced.

Mindy shook her head. "It doesn't matter. You're not old enough to make those kinds of adult decisions for yourself. He is an adult man, a leader in the church. He's supposed to protect children, not rape them."

The word still felt uncomfortable. It brought up visions of masked men grabbing women off the street at knife point. "But rapists don't tell their victims they love them," I argued.

Mindy cut me off. "Yes, they absolutely do. That's the way pedophiles groom girls to think what they are doing is okay. It isn't okay. You deserve better than that. Shame on your mother and on the whole community for blaming you."

Her words stayed with me, but like the memories, I pushed them away. I concentrated on studying and planning my new life without a husband and children. It was the first time I'd been allowed to consider a life different from Mem's. Brian said I would make a good accountant and brought me to his office where he repaired computers. His receptionist let me sit in her chair and showed me how to use a flow chart. When she walked away to help someone, I crossed my legs and picked up the phone, trying to cradle it on my shoulder and type at the same time. I looked down at my nails, bare and worn from biting. I would be the kind of woman who got regular manicures, the French kind, like Mindy. And I would get my diploma. Suddenly, I couldn't wait for my official life to begin. "I'm not like you, Mem," I thought. "I won't end up pregnant out of wedlock, forced to marry whoever feels sorry for me, and punishing my children for my mistakes. I won't be anything like you." I sat up straight, clasping my hands together on the desk, as if about to lead a meeting. I felt ready for anything.

* * * * *

By Christmas, I was broke again and found it hard to keep up in my classes. There was too much I didn't know. If anyone paid me attention, it was to make fun of me, and I spent most of my time hiding in the back row of the classroom, hoping no one would call me fat. Then Titus called. He and Uncle Marty had left the Amish and were driving to Ohio to look for jobs. He told me that I should come with them. The invitation took me by surprise, but I was glad to hear from the boy who smiled at me with big buck teeth back at the barn-raising frolic. His familiar voice felt like warm tea, dissolving the trapped feeling in my chest. He said he'd been missing me, but he needed to leave the Amish before he could tell me all of the details. He was free now, he quickly explained, to choose anyone he wanted. Talking to Titus didn't bring back the same butterflies I'd had years ago, but I wanted a taste of the freedom he was offering. I'd never before been free to do what I wanted. I began to daydream about Titus and Ohio.

On Christmas Eve in the middle of the family party, I told Brian and Mindy I was going away for the school break. We all got to open one present from the pile under the tree. I'd never seen so many presents under such a big pine tree covered with lights. I'd checked all the gifts for labels with my name on it and counted seven, the same number as all the other kids. I tried to imagine Mindy at the mall picking out seven presents for me, passing each store thoughtfully, thinking about what would make me happy. Seven whole times she chose something with me in mind. I'd been a family member, but never felt like part of a family until now. Mindy chose a flat box with my name on it and came to sit next to me on the sofa. It was wrapped in gold paper and tied with a matching ribbon. I stared at the small bow, not wanting to pull and destroy the perfect little treasure in my hand. "Open it," Mindy urged. I unwrapped it carefully, folding the paper and bow to save. It was a manicure set just like Mindy's with three shades of nail polish. "Now, I can show you how to do your own nails, and we can have spa days at home." Mindy beamed, but I started to cry. "Oh honey, what's the matter?" She put her arm around me.

"Thank you," I said.

"Of course. We love you."

Brian leaned down and kissed the top of my head then ruffled my hair. "Merry Christmas, kiddo." I tried to smile. They were giving me everything I'd always wanted. But as happy as I was with Brian and Mindy, I was unhappy with myself. I would never be good enough for the English. But I would never be good enough for the Amish, either. I was stuck in between. Alone. Soon, Brian and Mindy would come to their senses, and their charitable feelings would run out. I could still disappoint them. At least my family already knew the real me.

Titus and Marty were already on their way to pick me up, I told Brian and Mindy. They agreed reluctantly. "As long as you're back before school starts," they said. But I felt uncertain. Something inside me had changed. As much as I had tried to create, with Mindy and Brian, the happy childhood I had always wanted, that innocent spark was gone. While I loved being part of this happy English family, I often felt I was going through the motions, secretly counting the minutes until I could break away and be alone again. I hid my depression with sleep, which Brian and Mindy chalked up to normal teenage behavior. During my worst moments, I felt my childhood was over, that there was no use trying to pretend these kind people were my family, and that there was no chance I could ever graduate from high school. I told myself that opportunity died a long time ago in a freezing cold barn.

Mindy protested. "At least open the rest of your presents before you go," she urged. I looked at the packages under the tree that I knew were intended for me. Titus had said I could bring one small bag.

"Save them for me," I told Mindy. "I can open them when I get back." I figured when she realized I was gone for good, she would want her presents back anyway.

Two cars showed up to take me to Ohio. Titus and Marty were in one, and a bunch of former Amish I didn't know were in the other. Brian walked up to both and introduced himself, offering a handshake to each man and looking them in the eye. "I expect you all to bring her home safe," he said. Mindy stood beside him, biting her perfect nails. "They care so much," I thought. "What am I doing?" But Marty had already pulled away, out of their driveway. Brian and Mindy shrank away behind us.

Ohio was a blur. We drove there, got stuck in a ditch, and slept in a cornfield. Two of our companions stole food and liquor from an Amish farmhouse, and we ran from the cops. The only thing that kept me sane was Titus. I felt safe by his side the entire time. But at the end of three days, I was ready to go back. I thought about calling Brian and Mindy, but I felt ashamed and unworthy of them. High school was hard to take, and my dream of college seemed remote. Titus had no such expectations of me. He assured me he would return to Canton, but live as English. And he would wait for me.

Titus and I kept each other awake whenever it was his turn to drive through the night. With everyone else fast asleep in the seat behind us, it was hard not to feel close to him. The quiet world slipped past the windows, as if we were the only people in it. "It's hard to live on your own in the English world if you don't have experience," he cautioned me. "Just two more years back with your Mem and Datt, and you'll be eighteen. Then, we can do whatever we want."

Titus was saving up to start his own business and his own family. I sat next to him with my hands clasped neatly in my lap, listening to his plans. He put one hand on mine and continued staring at the road. His own family. It sounded nice and safe. For a moment, the sleeping butterflies awoke and fluttered gently against my stomach. Away from the Amish church, we could have any curtains we wanted, I thought. I pictured the open windows, a breeze gently causing the butter-yellow curtains to flutter. I imagined a little girl looking out the window, wearing a soft pink robe. No *over-kapp*, no apron, no *Ordnung*. I squeezed his hand.

My skin tingled with excitement, not in the same messy way as when Maverick kissed me, but with anticipation of things finally being okay. It's all I wanted: to feel okay again with someone who accepted me. Maybe Titus didn't know everything about me, but I could still be a good woman to him. As if reading my thoughts, Titus released my hand and laid his arm across my shoulders. I'd never felt so safe in my life. I closed my eyes and leaned my head against his arm, smiling as I thought of seeing Royal. I'd been away from home for six months. "Home," I thought. "Maybe it'll be different this time."

So, I ended up going back where I thought I'd never go again. Back to Mem and Datt and the *Ordnung*.

XIV
Canton, MN
January 1991

Mem and Datt said little about my time away. Royal seemed especially happy to pretend I'd never left. I took my time putting my Amish dress and apron back on. My fingers fumbled over the straight pins, as if my hands had grown too big for the delicate task. The bobby pins attaching my cap, which had never bothered me before, suddenly stabbed and scratched my scalp. I glanced at the open window in the bedroom, still covered with the dull blue curtains, briefly wondering if I could escape again. But where would I go this time? No one would help me again. I quickly turned back to straightening the pleats of my dress, determined to try. Just two more years.

One of Mem's conditions for my return home was that I go to a "chiropractic clinic," where I could work out my "emotional issues." So a few days after I came back, Mem, Datt, Aunt Iva, and I loaded onto a bus for South Dakota. The bus was filled with other Amish people all going to a "magic clinic" that treated Amish, from infants to elders, "for all kinds of ailments," Mem explained. Patients and their families stayed in hotel rooms above the clinic. Mem and Datt shared one bedroom while I slept in a small, adjoining living area with Aunt Iva, who was supposed to keep a close eye on me so I wouldn't run away during the night. A doctor sat with Mem and me for an intake interview as Mem explained I had "issues" that forced me to run away from home. The doctor, an English man in a tweed jacket, seemed to know what Mem meant by "issues." He asked some general questions about my health, made some notes, and gave me some pills right then and there in his office to help me sleep when I got home.

We stayed for five days. Each day, I went to the clinic for a deep massage, where a man asked me to lean into a massage chair. Mem sat in a chair in the corner. His hands crept over my dress and dug into my body, and I shut my eyes, trying to escape. I was getting better at leaving my own body. Once the appointment was done, we passed the rest of the day fishing or reading. I was used to being busy, not sitting around, but by the third day, I started to enjoy being away from everything. Datt and I spent rare time alone together on the lake. He showed me how to improve my line toss. It'd been so long since he'd first shown me, so long since we'd been together like this. Neither of us said much. We never brought up why we were there. It was nice that way: the simplicity of being together, as if I were a child again and there was nothing to talk about except the length of fishing line and the way it rippled through the water.

* * * * *

Once we returned from the clinic, we never spoke about it again, although I heard Mem call me damaged goods when talking to Datt one night in the kitchen. Royal continued to treat me as if nothing had ever happened, but I felt scared to be around her as if my sin with Aden was contagious. I wanted to protect her. So, I lashed out at her instead, yelling at her when she asked questions. I was too old to play with her, I said. *Leave me alone*!

Datt began bringing my brothers on delivery trips too long for the horse to travel roundtrip in one day. When he stayed out overnight, Mem did, too. Royal now worked as a *maude*, and without her, nighttime began to feel very lonely. With my future so uncertain, all I had to think about was the past. The shame and guilt I had begun to shed in LaCrosse crept back in, like a shadow, eventually consuming me again. The neighbors at *Gma* stared and whispered when they saw me, turning their backs instead of greeting us. They even shunned Royal, who'd done nothing wrong except to have the bad luck of being related to me. Still, it didn't seem to bother her. She disliked those girls anyway, she assured me, and stuck out her tongue when they sneered in our direction.

One night when Datt was away, Uncle Marty pulled his new pickup truck into our driveway, headlight brights on and the radio blasting. Mem, ready to go, stopped at the front door and glanced back at me. I was headed upstairs to read a Danielle Steele novel for the third time. It was the only thing I had in the otherwise empty house to keep the dark thoughts at bay. "You can come if you want," Mem said. "Titus will be there."

Titus and Uncle Marty stayed in touch with many of their Amish relatives—but they did so mostly through secret house parties in the middle of the night. Bored, lonely, and partly curious, I couldn't resist the invitation. Mem hopped between Uncle Marty and another man in the front seat. I sat in the back seat between two more men, and we took off for the town of Harmony.

Once on the road, Mem's personality changed. She let go of the quietly fuming, strict woman who fussed over Datt. The hints of wicked smiles I'd seen over the years that threatened to warm her icy demeanor finally broke free and changed the landscape of her face. She laughed louder and held her head higher. But it was not a comfort to me. I didn't see friendliness in Mem's new, relaxed eyes. I saw a stranger, someone I was afraid to become. Maybe Mem was right. Maybe I was just like her.

We parked in front of a small farmhouse. Mem hid our *kapps* in the glove compartment. I watched her eyes in the rearview mirror as she nervously straightened her hair. "What is she nervous about?" I wondered. But Mem walked through the front door with a swagger I'd never seen on her before. The more confidence she exuded, the more I wanted to disappear. The other men at the party, a mix of Amish and English, said they were from Ohio. They hovered over their cans of beer, shifting positions, moving slightly behind or to the side of me, just out of sight, but close enough to keep me alert. I thought Mem would surely notice if one got too close and give them a piece of her mind. But where was she? I tried to stay close to Titus, following close behind him as he wandered about the party. Marty joked that Titus better watch out—a man could find himself stuck with a wife that way.

Someone handed me a wine cooler, which tasted like bitter soda. But I quickly got used to it, and then the drinks went down faster. Mem flitted about from man to man, laughing and touching them as if she'd known them all her life. They seemed fascinated by her, vying for her attention as she beat them at cards, leaning in so she could touch their collars or swat their forearms, her fingers lingering playfully. As she declared victory on a round, an older man pulled her onto his lap. She cackled as he told her he was going to punish her for cheating. He whispered in her ear, and then they headed up the stairs. A chill went through me, and I felt frozen in place. I wasn't surprised that Mem was cheating on Datt. I already knew that about her. But I felt disappointed she would be so brazen about it. It was hard to see her leaving for short periods of time with random men at the party. She disappeared into an upstairs room, and suddenly I no longer mattered. Or maybe I never had. Titus looked over at me and said, "Let's go out to the bonfire."

Taking me by the hand, he led me out of the kitchen and away from the house. Across the road, bright orange flames snapped at the dark, lighting our way. His warm, calloused hand over my shivering fingers calmed me, and I began to feel happy as we stumbled and laughed, tipsy from the alcohol. More people gathered around the fire, drawn from another party at a neighboring farmhouse. A woman in jeans and a tank top handed me another bottle from a cooler, eyeing my ankle-length dress and lace-up boots with curiosity. Before I could take a sip, my stomach rolled. I gagged and lurched forward. The woman caught my arm. I'd never been sick outside before, and certainly never in front of strangers. I pushed her away and got sick in the tall grass.

"Gross," someone said. "Who is that, anyway?"

"Isn't she from Twisted Sister?" They laughed.

"Leave her alone," the woman said. "She's Amish."

Titus and Marty had to prop me up to walk back to the house. They let me lie on the sofa while we waited for Mem. Eventually, she shook me awake, and we went back home.

When we weren't partying, Mem and I went through the motions of being Amish. I tried to be obedient, but it was hard when I had just seen her screwing two random men at a party. I participated in the "Young People Singing" group at church, which was mandatory for boys and girls when they turned sixteen-and-a-half. While we were officially there to sing hymns, its actual purpose was for Amish teenagers to socialize with limited adult supervision. I sat there, bored, with a stiff, strained smile One of the boys poked me. It was Nathanial, asking if his younger brother, Isaac, could take me home for *snitz*. He gave me no chance to decline.

"It's settled," he said. "I'll let you know when Isaac is ready." I stared down at my hands, unable to look at the boys sitting on the other side of the kitchen because I was worried my eyes would meet Isaac's. The singing finally ended, and I went out to the washhouse to get my shawl and *over-kapp*, then walked slowly back to the buggies. Isaac waved me over, and I sat as close as I could to the far edge of the seat. "Tuck in the buggy robe tight. The wind is cold tonight," he said. He scooted close to me until his thigh rubbed up against mine and told the horse, "*Giddyup*, Tony!"

I crept up the stairs to my room, lit my kerosene oil lamp, and adjusted it to a low flame, as my cousins had instructed. I took off my church dress, leaving on my under-dress. In the bottom dresser drawer, I found the special cover-up that Mem had helped me sew to cover my arms. It was the only part she had ever explained to me about *snitz*. My cousins had told me about the bundling, too, so I untied the laces of my high-heeled *Gma* boots and kicked them under the bed at the last moment, remembering to leave my socks on. I climbed under the covers and slid against the wall. Maybe he won't come up, I thought.

But then I heard footsteps climbing up the stairs and echoing down the hallway. I peeked out to see him pushing aside the curtain that was my door. Isaac looked very serious as he yanked off his coat and shoes and blew out the lamp. The bed creaked as he climbed in beside me, and I froze, briefly wishing the wall would crumble so I could escape. Isaac reached over and pulled me flat against him, so that we were chest to chest and nose to nose. His breath came out in nervous puffs on my cheek as he wrapped his arms around my back and jerked from side to side. My cousins had said this bundling, hugging and rocking side-to-side all night, created the intimacy needed for romance. I quickly realized that bundling all night would be uncomfortable and awkward. When Isaac tried to kiss me, I pretended to fall asleep. Finally, he stopped rocking and started to snore.

Isaac left before sun-up, whispering promises of another date. I rolled over and forgot about it. But Isaac didn't forget. He came over a week later, crept into my room and found me with his brother, Nathanial, the older and more rebellious of the two. Isaac ran from the house, devastated. Years later, I wrote him a letter apologizing and asking for forgiveness. His wife wrote back and said they'd both forgiven me.

* * * * *

I was seventeen. Just one more year before I could legally leave the Amish for good. I had begun teaching in the same one-room schoolhouse where Royal, Wayne, my cousins, and I used to play together. But in the meantime, conforming to the expectations for a young Amish woman was harder than I'd expected. This reality became painfully clear at a neighbor's wedding. All the young folks were ushered into a shed. The girls and boys sat across from each other on opposite sides of the shed. In the corner, a dozen married Amish men sat smoking pipes, staring at us. I sat uneasily, shifting in the rickety chair, wondering if this was a game I had once heard rumors about. A boy ran up to me and snapped his fingers in my face, indicating that it was my turn to chase him. So, I did, quickly tagging him. The second I touched him, he stopped and planted a wet, sloppy kiss on my lips, then left me free to chase another boy. We had to play this game while the men laughed, cheered, and high-fived each other. Then we had to line up for the Black Room.

Two young men called "hustlers" pushed me through a curtain and into a dark room. Inside, a stranger grabbed me and pressed against me, kissing me. It was too dark to see to whom the hand or mouth belonged. I had to stay in there for five long minutes until the hustler yelled, "Next!" I pulled away, but the boy in the dark with me explained that he was the one leaving and I had to stay. The curtain moved aside, and a new boy came in, closing the curtain behind him. This boy was shyer, and instead of groping me, politely asked where I was from and how I was related to the married couple. Those five minutes went by much faster. Finally, they let me out and pushed a new girl inside. The hooting and hollering men applauded my exit, commenting on who I'd been coupled up with and asking what they had done with me. I was mortified. Why they were cheering for this was just beyond me.

* * * * *

I'd been buying English clothes at garage sales and stashing them in the back of my drawer to wear when I snuck out at night. Once, as I was leaving through the side door to meet up with some English friends, I turned to find Datt blocking my path. He glared at me for a moment, his eyes adjusting to the dark, trying to see if he knew this stranger in his driveway. I must've looked like an English girl in my stonewashed jeans and leather jacket, with my hair loose for everyone to see. He straightened up, his mouth buckling into a frown, and told me to get every item of clothing Mem would disapprove of and bring it to his shop. If I tried to keep anything, he'd know, and I'd lose my Amish clothes, too.

I brought them to his shop where he waited with a large pair of scissors. Without saying a word, he watched me, as one by one I shredded the jeans and t-shirts. When the pile was gone, Datt motioned to the clothes I was wearing. I couldn't bear the thought of destroying my favorite leather jacket, but I knew I had to. I started to cry. The tears were genuine, but I also hoped Datt would take pity on me and let me keep the jacket. Datt's expression remained unchanged. I reluctantly pulled it off and tried to cut through the thick leather. The scissors caught on the cuff and wouldn't budge. Datt held the sleeve taut, insisting I keep cutting until the jacket lay on the floor in pieces. "All of it," he said, looking at the low collar of my shirt where it met the beginning of my cleavage. I felt my face flush, but quickly removed my shirt and jeans, just wanting it to be over. I stood there, my body coiled tight in my bra and underwear, waiting for him to say the words: "You can go." But instead, Datt mumbled, "Do you want to mess around?"

"No!" I heard the word come out of my mouth without realizing I had said it. It sounded like someone else's voice, someone else's word. I turned, wrapping my arms around my chest, and hurried from the shop. I ran to the outhouse and locked the door. Cold sweat drenched my body. I shivered, hot and cold at the same time. I closed my eyes and drifted away, hovering somewhere in between consciousness and dreaming. Afraid of both.

XV
February 2018

S ome memories are too painful and confusing to write about. I have no answers to my questions, and neither do Mem and Datt. In those restless moments, I get up and venture into the attic corners where I shoved the boxes I most want to forget. One by one, I smooth out newspaper clippings and documents, looking for the DNA test that proved Datt wasn't my biological father. I had been told by Aden that Datt was not my biological father, but I was sixteen when I first went searching for answers. Rummaging in Mem's dresser one night, I found a book called *Abandoned Prayers* about Eli Stutzman, an infamous Amish serial killer. Mem caught me reading it that same night, but instead of getting angry, she became nostalgic.

She snatched it from my hands, then flipped through the pages, stopping at pictures of the man she met the year she left the Amish to live *Hoch* (high life among the English). Mem tightened her lips and fought back her tears as she turned to a dog-eared page. I was surprised, because I rarely witnessed her emotions. "This is not accurate. This is not the Eli I knew." She looked down at his picture with a faraway smile. "He was very handsome in his own way." I turned away as her fond memories of Eli Stutzman lightened her mood. I had no interest in hearing about her warm feelings for a man suspected of murdering his wife and son. It occurred to me that she'd known this man when she got pregnant, right before she returned to the Amish and married Datt. She gave birth to me four months later.

Could this be my father? "Ask Mem!" I scolded myself. But I never asked.

* * * * *

Up in the attic, I find the DNA report inside an old dictionary, where I must have tucked it back in 2001. Datt had finally agreed to the test a few years after

Mem left him and the Amish Church for good. Three more DNA tests ruled out three more men, but Mem said she was suspicious of the results. She must've drank a little too much and blacked out, she said. Someone must have "taken advantage" of her.

Although I remained determined to find my birth father, I was secretly relieved because it made those memories of Datt's bad behavior toward me slightly more bearable. It wasn't until his death from cancer in 2015 that I fully forgave him.

As usual, Datt said little when I told him about the DNA results. And when I asked him if he knew who my father could be, he just looked at the floorboards and shook his head.

XVI
January 1992

*i*n the end, Royal and I left the Amish not because of Aden or Mem or Datt, not because of Uncle Abe or Aunt Iva. We didn't leave over *snitzing* or creepy wedding games. We left over the color of a dress. A cousin asked Royal to make sure that we wore black dresses to the next *Gma*, as it was Rhoda's time of the month. We only wore all black in mourning or during our time of the month to show solidarity with each other. That way, no one could tease one girl; they'd have to tease all of us. Royal and I showed up on Sunday wearing black as planned, but as we walked in, we could see right away no other girls wore black dresses. I could feel Royal tense up beside me. They had not saved us seats either, instead they whispered and mocked us as we passed.

Royal's cheeks flushed bright red against her pale skin. She glared at the girls with such intensity that I began to squirm in my seat. I knew only that I was glad I wasn't on the receiving end of Royal's disdain, and that if I were, I'd be very afraid. I could see the girls struggling to remain composed under Royal's stare. I found myself wondering what else Royal was capable of. Her face looked eerily serene and enraged at the same time, like she was ready to conquer anything or anyone in her way. At that moment, I knew I would be safe. I realized Royal would be there to protect me, as she had been all along. We hadn't known our power, but maybe we'd had it the whole time.

As soon as the service ended, Royal snatched up her black shawl and *over-kapp* and stormed out. I froze, unsure what to do. Rhoda turned to look at me, but when our eyes met, she quickly looked away. I thought maybe Royal would come back. Perhaps she'd gone to the outhouse to cool off. I went to the window and pushed aside the heavy blue curtain. I could see Royal already walking past the outhouse at the end of the driveway. It was over three miles back home. Surely, she'd come back or at least wait for me to pick her up in the buggy. Someone called my name, and I turned to take a bowl of bread from the kitchen to the table where the men were waiting. When I came back to the window, I could no longer see Royal. The road was empty.

I went through the motions, put food on a plate, and stood holding it like a prop, unable to eat. I pretended not to notice as the girls in green giggled behind my back, then greeted me with masks of fake smiles, no trace of the friendship I'd once thought so secure. I felt like a stranger. Royal was the only thing that felt like home, and Royal was gone. Yet here I was standing in someone else's kitchen with people who disliked me, pretending to eat their food. I left without saying my goodbyes. I gave my uneaten food to the cats and headed home to Royal.

She was waiting for me, balled up in the corner of the bed, pouting. As soon as I came up the stairs, she exploded with energy, standing on the bed, her hands clenched into fists. "Am I invisible?"

"Of course not," I said. "I can see you right there." I turned around to change my clothes.

A pillow hit the back of my head. "Then how come no one sees me?"

"Royal!" I looked up. Her face looked the same as it had the day she was born, the same eyes, the same scrunched-up nose, the same stubborn expression. I couldn't stay mad at her. She'd seen me change from a fun, loving older sister to a scared, angry stranger.

"Of course I care. Stop being an old heifer."

Royal looked as though flames might come roaring from her mouth. "Don't you call me that. You're not Datt, and neither of us is an old heifer! But not one person asked me what was wrong, not even you. It's like I don't exist."

I sighed, "I'm sorry, Royal."

With her hands on her hips and her feet firmly planted, Royal reminded me of the image of God I'd once lived by—Paul Bunyan standing ten feet tall, full of strength, ready to strike. "What would you do if I left? Who would even talk to you? No one."

"You're right."

"You probably wouldn't even go looking for me."

"Of course, I'd look for you." Royal was silent. She crossed her arms and looked over my head, unwilling to believe me. "I'd never stop looking for you," I continued. "I'd walk forever and ever until I found you." I searched Royal's face for a sign she was listening, but she locked her knees, refusing to budge.

Royal had the same look on her face as I'd seen at *Gma* earlier: proud and strong. Utterly unafraid. "I'm leaving for good. Are you coming with me, or are you going to stay here like the old heifer you are?"

I didn't hesitate. "I'm coming with you."

Royal looked skeptical. "You don't realize that all the time, I was going through it with you. I knew you were suffering, and there was nothing I could do. I was hurting, too, Lizzy. But don't you see? Now I can do something."

She collapsed onto the bed beside me, and we curled up together, pulling the blanket over our heads the way we used to when we were little, pretending we were orphans and the blanket was our shelter. Our bed was the woods. And all we had was each other.

The next day, I called Cherry from the payphone in Canton, and she agreed to pick us up the following Tuesday. Mem would be away that evening with the boys. Datt would be busy in the shop. Royal and I spoke very little during the last few days, as if we might give ourselves away just by being noticed. Between us, we had $25, a hairbrush, two books, and our journals. We left our clothes behind, they would be worthless in the English world. I'd never have to wear a milk-stained apron or pleated bonnet again.

I surged with excitement, taking extra care with my chores, appreciating that I could milk a cow if I ever needed to in the English world. I could make my own clothes and grow my own food. I could hunt, I could build, I could survive. I could and would do all these things, but now I was getting out for good. I was excited for my relationship with Titus. I had Royal, and I had something new: freedom, choices. We thought that life might now go exactly the way we wanted it to. But it didn't. We walked out the door, but it would never close neatly behind us.

We waited until after supper. Datt slid his chair away from the table just like any other night. He put on his coat and patted the pockets to make sure his pipe and tobacco were inside. He looked back at his daughters, already starting their chores, not knowing they'd be gone by morning. Then he headed out the door, shutting it tight against the wind behind him. Royal and I watched him walk away, a tiny shadow against the massive land and sky around him.

Just after sunset, we crept down the stairs, barely breathing, and out the back door. The house was empty, but when the screen door squeaked, my heart jumped into my throat. Royal paused before stepping outside. Was she waiting for me to stop her from making a huge mistake? Would God punish her for my sins? I stopped. My hand gripped the door handle. Now that I had to close it behind me, it felt impossible to let go. Royal whispered, "You don't have to worry, Lizzy. God told me He's right here, walking beside us." My knees felt weak, and my feet were paralyzed, unable to take the last step. Royal looked up the road and smiled. "Let's go," she urged. The fear broke, and I let go of the door.

We stepped down onto the icy grass and clasped hands. I hesitated for only a moment, reaching back to make sure the door was shut. I could hear the wind howling through rotted crevices of old wood, and the hinges of the screen door screeching as it banged in the cold: open, closed, open, closed. We began to run, up over the hill, past the shop where Datt was smoking his pipe, toward the fence and the road that would take us far away. I could hear the house rattling as we ran, as if pleading for us to return.

It would be 26 years before we did.

Photographs and Ephemera

LIZZY'S FIVE YEAR DIARY
"The summer I turned fourteen, Mem gave me a diary, a small book of lined pages with a red leather cover and a gold lock."

ENTRIES FROM LIZZY'S DIARY FROM 1989.
LATER, SHE SCRIBBLED OVER THE RECORDS OF RAPE BY ADEN,
FINDING IT DIFFICULT TO BE CONFRONTED BY THE EVIDENCE

MEM'S DIARY

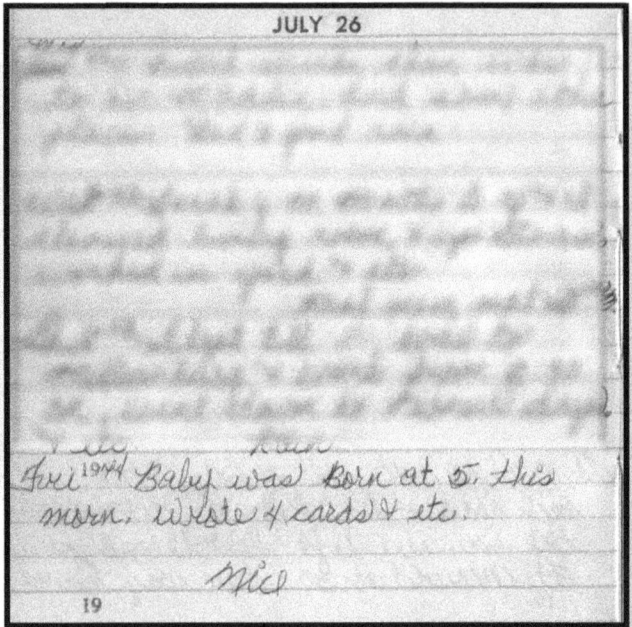

JULY 26

Jul 1974 Baby was born at 5. this morn. wrote & cards & etc.

19

MEM'S DIARY ENTRY ON THE DAY LIZZY WAS
BORN, PROLOGUE

THE AMISH ARE FORBIDDEN FROM TAKING PHOTOGRAPHS, SO THERE
ARE NO BABY PICTURES OF LIZZY. AN EARLY PICTURE TAKEN IN 1979 OF
LIZZY AGE 5, WITH MEM HOLDING HER BROTHER, AND ROYAL AGE 4

EARLIEST KNOWN PHOTO.
BACK ROW: ROYAL, AGE 3,
AND LIZZY, AGE 4 WITH
THEIR COUSINS

LEFT TO RIGHT: 1983, LIZZY, MEM, ROYAL

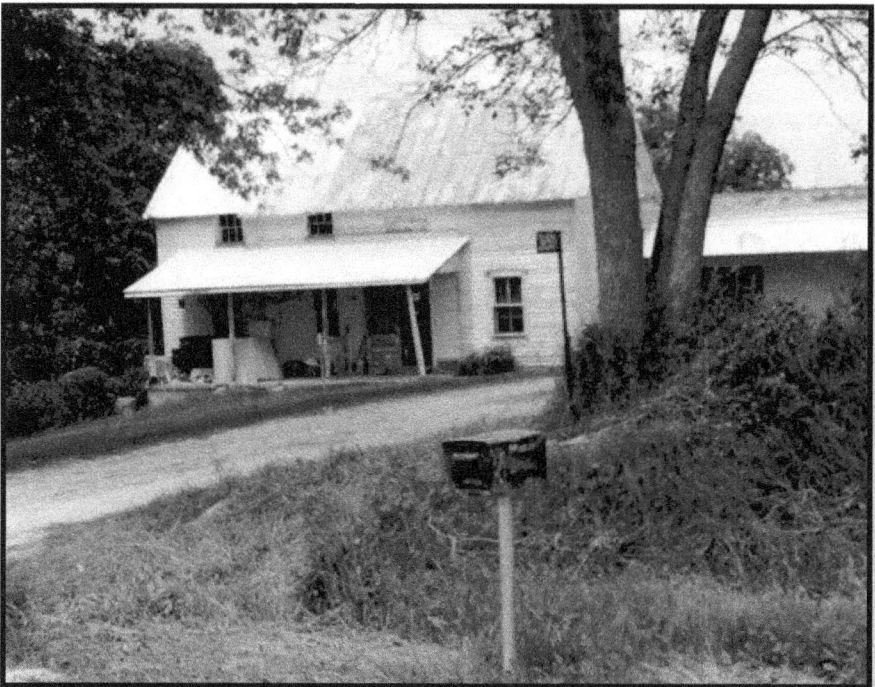

THE HOUSE THAT LIZZY GREW UP IN, CANTON, MN, CHAPTER I

LIZZY, AGE 9, WITH HER HAIR UNBRAIDED BY ROYAL
BEFORE MEM WASHED AND RE-BRAIDED IT, CHAPTER VI
"Oh, how my eyes would well up with tears from the tight braiding!"

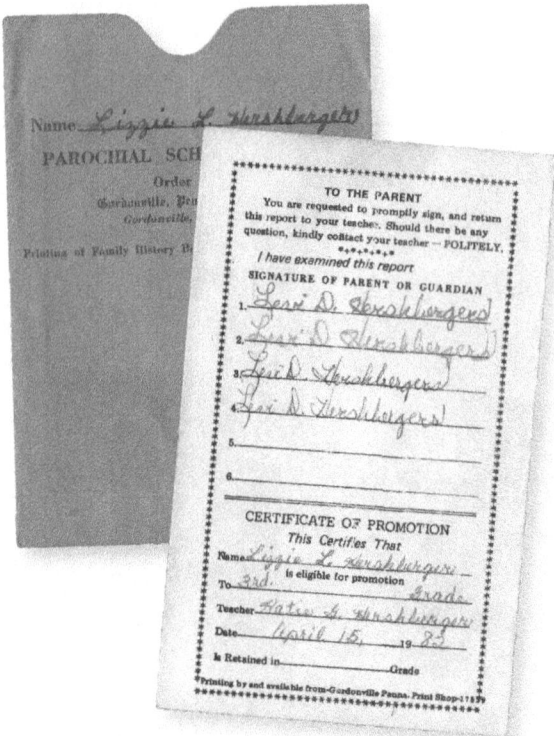

LIZZY'S THIRD GRADE REPORT CARD,
CHAPTER VI
*"We walked to school barefoot along the edge of the short
gravel road, our lunch buckets swinging by our sides."*

LIZZY, AGE 9

THE COW BARN AND THE HORSE BARN AT MUMMY
AND DODDIE'S FARM, CHAPTER IV
*"Uncle Abe leaned over and whispered in my ear. "Never tell anyone what happened here, or
more terrible things will be coming your way."*

Minneapolis Star and Tribune   Sat., Oct. 15, 1983   . 9A

Staff Photo by Bill McAuliffe

The fire apparently started in a bedroom on the main floor of the farmhouse near Canton, Minn.

Fire Continued from page 1A

CLIPPING FROM THE *MINNEAPOLIS STAR AND TRIBUNE*,
10/15/83 ABOUT THE FIRE , CHAPTER VIII
*"I'll never forget the cries of Aunt Vera, Mummy, and the cousins as
they lowered the two small caskets into the ground."*

AT HOME IN CANTON, MN, 1982. *CENTER TOP OF PYRAMID*: MEM, FLANKED BY ROYAL AGE 6 (*L*), AND LIZZY, AGE 8 (*R*). THE BROTHER HELD BY ROYAL WAS ONE YEAR OLD. THE BROTHER STANDING IN FRONT OF LIZZY WAS AGE 3. THE GIRLS WEARING SHORTS ARE COUSINS. MIKEY THE DOG IS TO THE BACK RIGHT.

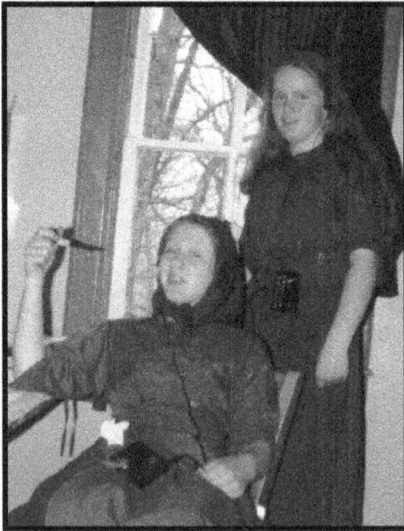

LIZZY (*L*) AND ROYAL (*R*). NOTE THE BLUE CURTAINS AND FORBIDDEN WALKMANS, CHAPTER XII
"Now be quiet, or I'll tell Datt about your Walkmans."

CASSETTE TAPE THAT ADEN GAVE LIZZY ALONG WITH A WALKMAN AFTER A FISHING TRIP, CHAPTER X
"I got you a Walkman." He reached under the seat and handed me a small black box with headphones. "When you listen to it, think of me."

LIZZY AGE 14, RIGHT BEFORE
SHE WENT TO WORK AS A *MAUDE*
FOR ADEN AND CEVILLA

LIZZY IN THE BUGGY DRAWN BY REX, GOING TO ADEN AND CEVILLA'S
HOUSE TO WORK, 1989, CHAPTER X

"...before I knew it, we were in the buggy, driving up the road to my new home."

LIZZY, AGE 15, SKATING AND SMOKING WITH
WAYNE TROYER AND HER BROTHERS AT
THE POND BEHIND HER GRANDPARENT'S FARM

LIZZY AGE 17 (*L*), AND HER FRIEND
RHODA (*R*) 10 DAYS BEFORE LIZZY
LEFT THE AMISH FOR GOOD

LIZZY AGE 15, IN ENGLISH CLOTHES
WHILE STILL LIVING AS AMISH

1990, LIZZY'S FIRST ATTEMPT AT
"JUMPING THE FENCE" (LEAVING THE
AMISH) CELEBRATING WITH A PERM BY
DARLENE'S DAUGHTER AND GARAGE-
SALE ENGLISH CLOTHES, CHAPTER XXII

DATT, 2005

DATT HEADED TOWARDS THE WORKSHOP,
HIS REFUGE, CHAPTER I
"Mummy left in a huff, and Datt went back to his shop."

PATERNITY TESTS FOR LIZZY, PROVING THAT DATT WAS NOT
HER BIOLOGICAL FATHER, CHAPTER XV
"As usual, Datt said little when I told him about the DNA results."

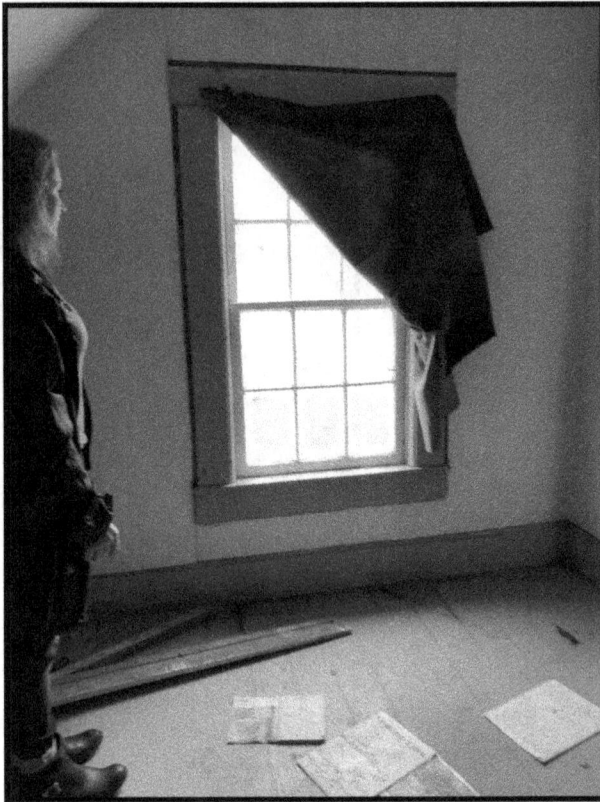

26 YEARS AFTER SHE LEFT, LIZZY IN HER OLD
BEDROOM IN CANTON, MN, CHAPTER XVIII
"Our room feels smaller and stuffier than I remember."

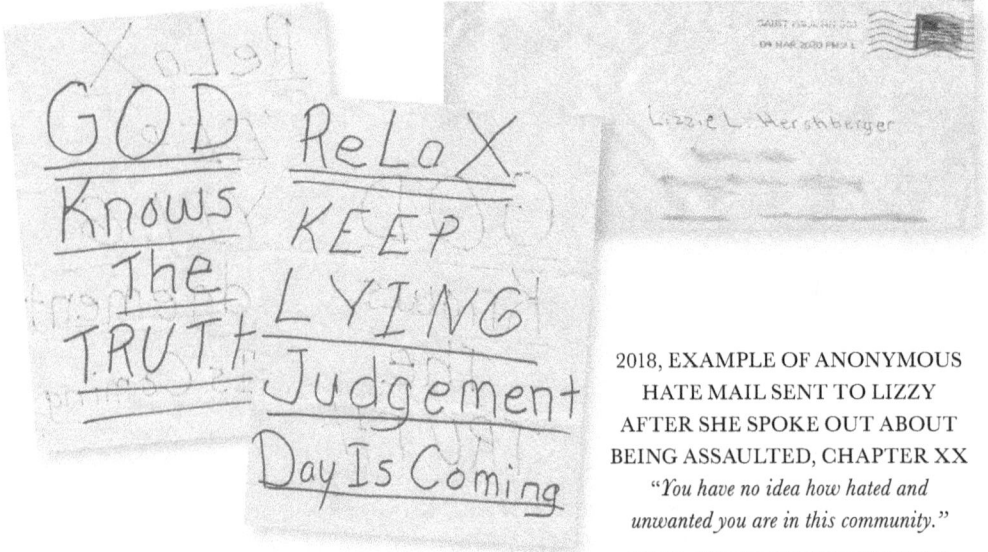

2018, EXAMPLE OF ANONYMOUS
HATE MAIL SENT TO LIZZY
AFTER SHE SPOKE OUT ABOUT
BEING ASSAULTED, CHAPTER XX
*"You have no idea how hated and
unwanted you are in this community."*

PART II

XVII
Canton, MN
June 2018

ochelle and DJ have friends over. They're playing games in the basement when I'm alerted by a sharp hush followed by lowered voices. I tiptoe to the basement steps and hear Rochelle urging her friends: "Don't talk about it."

Don't talk about it. Almost thirty years have passed. Yet Rochelle's words feel like a cold stone wall hitting my back, seizing the breath in my chest. They feel like Aden slamming me against the hayloft, like the buggy seat cracking against my hip bone, like the candy that wasn't in Uncle Abe's pocket, like the disgust on Mem's face.

I crouch at the top of the steps and hold my breath, listening.

"She sent him a picture on Snapchat."

"She was only wearing a bikini."

"That's how it started."

"They hooked up in her car."

The words sting in my ears. The boy that they're talking about is around DJ's age. The teacher is close to thirty. I think of my back slamming into the cold wall of the barn hayloft and the words equally as cold and hard, still lingering.

"I'm sure he loved every minute." Nervous laughter follows, like noisy alarm bells.

No one believed me. Why would anyone believe this boy?

I'm not just a bystander. I'm not like the community members and neighbors who knew that Aden was assaulting me and said nothing. I can't just walk away. I'm an adult now, a mother on the school board, expected to vote to renew the teacher's contract despite the rumors. Rumors. "That's all it is," my friends on the school board insist when they call to chat about the weather and the kids. But mostly they call to gossip and express their opinions on this gossip, which I'm expected to share and promote accordingly.

We sit together at our kids' football games and at church, intimate only in the physical spaces of rickety bleachers and church pews, never giving up more than the occasional complaint about our husbands or busy schedules. Rarely do we allow the truth to spill over the neat lines of what others are supposed to see. If we do, we always assure each other that God will never give us more than we can handle, and then express gratitude for our blessings. We talk about our kids, horses, and plants. The conversation shifts to how the teacher has already been transferred under similar circumstances a couple of times. An investigator has been asking questions, and the boy and his mother refuse to cooperate. His mom doesn't think it's a big deal, so we shouldn't either.

"She's happily married."

"You know how kids talk."

"I've known her for years."

"I told her she has nothing to worry about."

"She's the best teacher we've had in years."

"Vote to keep her!"

I've heard all this before. Different words, same sentiments, years earlier. Not Mem or Datt's voice, not the Amish voices. This is DJ's voice, Rochelle's voice, Titus's voice and my friends' voices. But where is my voice? Does it even exist? If it does, what would I say? I let their conversation drown into the sounds of a video game coming to life, then I creep away and check on Dusty, hoping he needs me so I can delay getting into the shower. I feel suddenly afraid to be alone, even in the bathroom. What will I hear when all the other voices fade away? When there's no voice telling me what to think? Dusty leans back and smiles when he sees me. I wave and wait for him to try and wave back, a soothing act that would help me feel like everything is okay. When he does, I glance at the phone, wishing it would ring, and that someone would call and tell me something, anything. Its silence seems to mock me.

Aden stole more than my virginity that night. He ripped out my voice, one I never even knew I had, one I didn't know could be taken away. How do you claim something was stolen if you never knew you had it in the first place? I brought up the accusations against the teacher with Titus. "It's not that different from what happened to me," I insisted. He knew only a little about Aden Slabaugh. Before we were married, we attended pre-marital counseling at a Mennonite church in Ohio. Eventually, I trusted our pastor and his wife enough to confide in them about Uncle Abe and Aden. I went to their office alone where I poured out my story for the first time, relieved to share my secret. The pastor's wife looked at her husband with such sad eyes, and for a moment, I thought she understood me. "Oh, those poor men," she said. "They must feel horrible about what they did."

The pastor nodded. "You must forgive them."

I thanked them and left, but inside I was seething. Even so, at the time, I thought they were right and took their advice. Now, all these years later, I wonder: How many women had shared similar abuse with their pastors? How many women heard those words?

"Relax," Titus says. I still cringe whenever anyone says that to me. I still hear echoes of Aden's voice in the hayloft. Relax. "No sense talking about it," Titus says. My voice, again unwelcome, silenced, squashed.

I shuffle to the bathroom, determined to remain numb and get through the mundane action of taking a shower, which takes more effort than it should. I force myself out of my clothes and into the tub. The water shoots violently from the shower head, the loud spray jarring me out of my fog and slashing at my skin like tiny daggers. I hold onto my body, wrapping my arms around my breasts and hips, afraid to let go, as if someone is watching. And then I can't let go, because if I do, I'll crumble like a neglected, ancient building, brick by brick, bone by bone, collapsing into a soft pile and slowly washing away down the drain until there's nothing left but clear running water and an empty tub.

The teacher would stay, perhaps to abuse again, and the kid would move on. And then what? He would do what he was supposed to do. Get good grades. Grow up. Have kids. Pretend it never happened. Soon I can't tell the difference between my tears and the drops of water hitting my face. I don't know if the water rushing down my arms comes from my eyes or the shower head. I've never pulled from the well of grief that has grown like a separate entity in my body. But now the grief slinks down through my core, wrapping around my organs until I can't tell the difference. They are one and the same. I'm not a crier. Titus doesn't like it, either.

My relationship with Aden was deceptive and confusing. That's what drew me in. The day after the rape in the barn, his hand fell softly on the back of my head. The warmth from his hand seeped into my scalp. His fingers gently brushed my hair away from my forehead. No one had ever touched me that way. Or maybe they had. It felt vaguely familiar, as if Mem had absent-mindedly soothed me to sleep while writing in her diary, or Datt had brushed his fingers over his beard while I lay sleeping in his lap. Royal had been affectionate as a kid, curling up against me on cold nights, but mostly she huddled into my back as I turned away from her, trying to get some sleep.

I try to remember if I was affectionate enough toward my own kids when they were younger. But I can't remember ever stroking Rochelle's head that way, nor Dusty, DJ, or Darrel. Certainly, I hug them if they cry, but I also encourage them to get back up and keep going. Now I'm not sure that was the right decision.

The boy is underage. I wonder, has the accused teacher ever sent Snapchats to DJ? Has any teacher ever sent pictures to Rochelle? Has anyone ever hurt them? The idea cramps my gut, and I sit down, the water hitting the back of my neck. I'm sure they would come and tell me if anyone was inappropriate. But why am I so sure? Am I so different from Mem? Sobs rack my body. I feel ashamed suddenly of my nude body, exposed somehow even in the privacy of the bathroom. I want to cover it up, and I try to swallow myself in my arms and bury my grief between my knees. I think I'll never be able to get up again, nor do I want to. I think surely, I can die right here.

Eventually, I rub my face raw with my hands, trying to wash the grief away, and stand up, exhausted. I get out and dry off. Catching a glance of myself in the mirror, I don't even recognize myself. My eyes are puffy and red. My face is white as a ghost. When I reach up to touch it, my skin is ice cold. Each time I hear about this teacher, I end up thinking about Aden. Then I remember the investigator at the Sheriff's department who handled the student/teacher accusations. I'd called him to hear his perspective. "I believe the victim," he'd said. It was the first time I'd heard anyone say that. Maybe I could talk to him.

I put on my flannel pajamas and fluffy pink robe, tying the belt tightly around my waist. I pull up the hood, snuggling it up over my head and letting my bangs fall over my face to hide my eyes. But I can't stop shaking. I limp to the office, sit down in front of my desk, and grab a pen. My fingers feel like icicles. I want to write down my thoughts before I lose courage. I want to leave evidence if something happens to me. Someone needs to know the truth and help the Amish children we left behind. My thoughts race. "They have no one to go to," I think.

What will happen to my marriage if I come forward to report this?

What will my kids say when they find out their mom was abused?

When can I tell them why I sacrificed so much to protect them?

I have always done everything I could to keep them safe from harm or abuse.

Rochelle's words echo in my ears. I hear her voice again and again: "I'm sure he loved every minute." It's me she's talking about; she's laughing at me. I get up from my chair and start pacing. Back and forth, back and forth. I hear the kids come up the stairs and start looking for snacks in the pantry. They have no idea I cried my eyes out in the shower, no idea I'd been raped in a barn, no idea how exciting it is to have someone pay attention to you the day after your rape, to make it seem so reasonable, to make you feel so dirty and so loved at the same time.

"Everything will be okay," my Amish girl voice says.

"But you're not okay," another voice answers.

XVIII
July 2018

O ne month later, Royal is the one who gently pushes me forward. Just as she did that night we left at the door of Mem and Datt's house, the night we left for good. We're standing in my kitchen talking about the school board meeting where I voted not to renew the teacher's contract. Royal bustles around me cleaning up anything out of place she can find: a crooked placemat on the counter, a speck of dust, a fork that needs rewashing. Her cheeks flush red. She stops and looks up. "Good for you, Lizzy! Someone needs to stand up for the children." She shakes her head and grabs the broom from the pantry for a second round of sweeping. I look at the clean floor, but I don't argue. Royal needs to feel useful like a diabetic needs insulin. She's not aware that I would never have survived without her, but it has nothing to do with her skills in the kitchen.

"Yes, someone needs to stand up for the children," I agree. Royal sweeps briskly, telling me how I've done the right thing. "We can't let Satan win." Her cheery voice rises and falls as she bends down to attend to dusty crevices in the floor that only she can see. I wander toward the screened-in porch, looking across the road. I don't know what I'm looking for, but I know where it is. "Let's go for a ride," I say. Royal bangs the broom, trying to shake loose some dirt to sweep into the dustpan. "Now?"

I snatch the broom away. "Yes, now."

Royal follows me out to the truck and hops into the passenger seat. We drive in silence. Royal looks out the window; I stare straight ahead. As I pull onto our old road and park in front of the chained gate, she sits up and clasps her hands, silently praying. I get out first and march up to the barbed wire fence, sizing it up so I can climb over. "Lizzy!" Royal calls out. She stands next to the fence surrounding the abandoned house and farm, stretching out the barbed wire on top to see if we can squeeze through. "I'll hold it open for you," she says. I manage to get through the fence with only a small nick to my jacket, then hold open the wire for Royal. Once we're both planted safely on the other side, Royal asks, "What now?" I don't answer, just walk to the back door and put my hand on the doorknob.

"Wait!" Royal rushes to stand behind me, putting her hand on my shoulder. "It must be locked," she whispers, although there's no one around to hear us. The house has been empty for years. The door creaks open and stops, as if inviting us in. Royal steps closer to me, her hand clutching my arm, her chin hovering above my shoulder. I wait until she takes a breath and push.

The door swings open, the shadows widen. There are the blue painted walls, still peeling toward the wood floors, now covered in dust and cobwebs. "Mem would have a heart attack," I say. Royal laughs, and I follow, the spell of our past broken for a moment. We walk inside, hesitant and slow, Royal's arms wrapped tight around her chest as I zip around pointing out where things used to be. I walk into Mem and Datt's old room. It's empty, except for the torn blue curtains still hiding the room in shadow.

We come to the bottom of the staircase, littered with flies and cobwebs. The door at the top remains closed. I take a step and feel Royal's hand on my back, warning me not to go further. I look back at her. "Come on," I say. But Royal shakes her head and steps back, folding her arms back around herself, silently letting me know she won't come with me. She will wait.

Our room feels smaller and stuffier than I remember. I can see everything exactly as it was: the bed, the dresser, the blue curtains. All of it is gone. I can hear Royal sniffling downstairs. I turn to leave. I'm not much of a hugger, but I want to comfort her with my presence. A streak of blue draws me to the window, a little Amish girl running across the schoolyard. I can see her in the distance, in front of the same schoolhouse I walked to every day. Her figure appears and reappears through the slats in the wooden fence. She's running from someone. I hear her scream, and I crane my head. But she's disappeared. The yard is quiet again. I run down the stairs, grab Royal's hand, and pull her through the back door. "What's the matter?" She chases after me as I run toward the road, searching for the blue dress.

Another scream pierces the air. "There!" I yell. "Listen." The screams tumble into high-pitched laughter.

"Aw, they're playing tag," Royal observes. "Aren't they cute?" The little blue dress is standing in a circle with other little blue dresses and a few miniature wide-brimmed hats. "Must be recess," she says.

The teacher comes to the door, and the sound of the kids fades away as they assemble back inside. "Who's going to stand up for them?" I ask. Royal and I stand together, arms crossed. I know that I don't have to explain, that I'll never have to explain to Royal. I could have told her everything. I could have run home all those years ago and scrunched in beside her and told her what Aden had done. Even when I'd returned to him the next day, I could've come back and told her again, and again, and again. She had never left me; they had taken her from me.

I grab her hand. "Royal, Aden raped me." She squeezes me back, watching my face as I cry. "I'm sorry." I feel like I'm about to collapse.

Royal puts an arm around me and holds me up. The school door is closed, the yard quiet. "You have nothing to be sorry for, Lizzy. They stole our innocence. They're the ones who should be sorry." I look back at her, aware that what we share more than anything else is Mem. Datt isn't my father, but he's definitely hers. I still don't know who my real father is, but I'd come to know that what Aden told me in the barn was true. Datt had sexually assaulted his *maude*s. Aden never loved me. There had been no candy in Uncle Abe's pocket.

"Did Uncle Abe … ?" I stop, unsure if it's okay to continue.

Royal nods. "And others." She loosens her grip, dabbing at my face with her sleeve.

I pull away. "What are we gonna do?" I ask. "He's still a deacon in their church. He still has access to those girls."

Royal holds onto my hands and turns to face me. We look at each other, the house right behind us, as if it's waiting for us to decide. The barn and Datt's shop still sit just beyond, empty, defeated. "Look," Royal says with a sweep of her arm.

"They have no power over us anymore. They can't tell us what to do." I stare at the door of the schoolhouse. I don't want to abandon them again. "I have to do something," I say.

"God will tell you what to do," Royal says. "They can't take God away from us."

By the time we get back, Royal says, "Don't worry. God told me what to do." She pats the sofa beside her and dials a number into her phone. She presses the speaker button. Before I can ask who she's calling, a calm voice answers. Royal introduces us. "This is Jane," she says. "She's a victim's advocate." Then Royal tells Jane my story as if she's practiced a hundred times. I'd said so little to her over the years, yet the words tumble effortlessly off her tongue. How does she know? I wonder. We hunch together over her cell phone, ear to ear, listening to Jane's advice. "It doesn't matter if it was thirty years ago or thirty minutes ago," Jane says, her voice like a large, flat rock, still in the chaos of our raging river. "He's a pedophile and he's probably still abusing girls." I gasp and cover my mouth as Royal agrees with Jane. But I can't contain myself. "He has grand-daughters that age," I yell. "He's probably doing the same thing to them!" Royal keeps nodding, but puts her finger to her lips, motioning to me that Jane is saying something important. She covers the phone with her hand and whispers at me, even though there's no one else around. "She says you should report him."

Royal offers me the phone. I can hear Jane's voice, more excited now, giving us instructions I'm not ready to hear. Royal sighs dramatically and holds the phone to my ear. And I listen.

XIX
July 2018

i 've never been inside the police station before. I park in the adjacent lot so no one will see my car next to the jail, and step inside. A woman at the front desk takes my name, and the investigator for the Sheriff's Office, Captain John De-George, comes through a security door to take me back to his office. He clears off the folding chair across from his desk and motions for me to sit. My back is facing the holding cell, and I'm unable to shake the sight of four men sitting inside staring at me. John's suit and tie, neatly trimmed hair, and a reserved smile balance out his boyish face. He sits and folds his hands in his lap, waiting for me to speak.

"I need to tell someone …" I stop, unable to finish, and cup my hands over my face to hide the coming tears. John gets up and closes the door. The din of the jail fades. I take a breath, determined not to waste his time. "I'm sorry," I say.

"It's okay," he says, setting a box of tissues in front of me. "Do you want to talk here? Or I can set you up with a victim's services advocate in a room where it's more private." The word "victim" hangs in the air, a word I'm not sure belongs to me. Then I remember hiding in the outhouse all those years ago—how cold and alone I felt. Surely, the word would belong to any other child in that situation.

"I'm okay now," I say, and hesitate. I try to measure how quickly I can get back to my car. I can still get up and say I'm in the wrong office. I can leave right now without saying a word. But instead I say, "I grew up Amish."

John picks up a legal pad and a pen and makes a note.

I think of my car again, worried that at any moment a neighbor will drive by, recognize it, and report me to the gossip mills. The thought of them keeps me rooted to my seat. "I left years ago," I continue. "I'm here to report the sexual abuse of Amish children."

"Amish children?" John asks. "Any particular child?"

I look down at my hands, noticing how worn they've become. "Yes."

John starts to write something, then stops. He clears his throat. "And who is the child?"

I sit up. I fight the urge to run. I have to look him in the eye for the words to come out. "The child is me."

John straightens his posture and moves closer to the desk. He sits perfectly straight as he takes notes, pausing to make eye contact when he has a question.

"State your full name."

"How old were you?"

"What is your date of birth?"

"What is the offender's name?"

"How old was he?"

* * * * *

It won't be long now before everyone hears the story on Aden and forms an opinion. I tell Titus. He stares at me across the kitchen, dumbfounded. "Why are we still talking about something that happened thirty years ago?"

"It's not something," I shoot back, startled by my harsh response. I lower my voice. "He raped me."

"But that's all in the past now. Why drag it all up? You're gonna put the kids and me through it, too?"

I sigh heavily and toss a dish towel into the sink. "Oh, Titus." I'm too tired to argue. I'd sacrificed everything for my family. Every decision I'd ever made was for them. I'd given the first seventeen years of my life to the Amish and then another twenty-eight to my husband and children. Sometimes I dreamed of running away from it all. I could, I would, keep going for my kids.

The second time I go in to talk with Captain John DeGeorge, I bring my diary with me. I try to forget the recording device on his desk as he takes me through the details. Afterwards, I sit in a separate room with a Victim's Services Advocate named Sarah, show her where I scribbled over the original sentences to hide what Aden had done, and cry tears I couldn't with John. She lets me show her the few photographs I have from my childhood. It was the first time I'd shown anyone my diary and told my story in such detail. While I was grateful for the emotional release, I couldn't stop worrying about who might see my car and what I would say if questioned.

John calls a few months later. "He admitted it," he says. "I'll come out to your house and explain."

John sits at the kitchen table across from Titus and me and tells us his deputies had been trying to find Aden for months, but he'd avoided them. Finally, a deputy went to Aden's house late at night to demand he set up an appointment. "He seemed remorseful, quiet, relieved that it had come out. He said he'd tried to put it behind him. When Cevilla arrived home during the interview, I asked Aden if he wanted to stop the interview. But he said 'no' and kept talking."

"What did Cevilla do?" I ask.

"Cevilla just paced around for a few minutes, listening, but then she left. He wants to have a meeting with you to apologize. Aden couldn't remember everything. But he said if you say it happened, he believes it must be true."

Titus listens, as if we're sitting around talking about what to have for supper. I start feeling guilty, like I'm just causing problems. But I also want people to hear the whole story. They all acted like it was no big deal. And it is a big deal.

But after Captain John DeGeorge leaves, I start thinking maybe I should've given Aden a chance to apologize before I reported him. Perhaps I should have done what I thought the Amish would want me to do: I go looking for Cevilla to have a heart-to-heart. Perhaps we can talk like two women, like mothers and not enemies. I'd heard that she worked in a winery, definitely breaking the *Ordnung*, advising tourists on the best local chardonnay to serve with fish. I sit on the edge of the bathtub, hunched over with the phone, hoping I have the wrong winery.

"Hello, can I talk to Cevilla?"

"Yep ... hold on." In a flash, she's on the phone. "Hello?"

Without thinking, I start speaking in Amish. "I'm *Jecky Lissy*."

Cevilla's voice remains flat, unaffected. "Oh."

Flustered, I search for the right words. "The investigator told me that Aden suggested we all meet in person, so he can apologize."

"No!" Her voice feels like a quick jab. "There's absolutely not gonna be a meeting."

I can feel the Amish girl in me backing away, unsure of herself. "I'm sorry now that I reported it. I should've told you first. I feel bad that your kids learned this about their dad." I wait for a sign of forgiveness, but she responds with icy silence. "Are they doing okay?" I stammer.

"No!" She snaps again. "My kids found out before he was even questioned. My kids were NOT supposed to find out about this."

"Well, don't worry about it," I continue. "There aren't going to be charges. It happened too long ago. There's nothing to worry about."

Cevilla knows she has me in her grasp. "Well, we've already heard the cops were out in the community asking about his character."

"Nothing's gonna happen," I insist.

Cevilla laughs, a dry cackle. "Whatever happens, it won't be good for you. I can promise you that." Then she hangs up.

I find out it won't be my decision, after all. In March 2019, the Fillmore County Attorney decides for me and independently moves forward on the case against Aden. Assistant County Attorney Marla Stanton calls me into her office. She's sharp and professional, the kind of woman I once imagined I would be.

"I'm ready to proceed with charges," she says. "Four counts of first-degree sexual assault. Technically, he was your employer and that makes this a crime we are legally still able to pursue. Are you prepared to testify if this goes to trial?"

"Absolutely." The word comes out before I feel comfortable with the thought. The Lizzy I know is too afraid to take this on. But this is bigger than me, and I'm ready for them to put me on the stand. I want to describe in detail exactly what happened because his side of the story is still the only side most people have heard. Just a brief affair. A mistake. And to them, that was okay. Now I know it wasn't okay and never would be. I'm ready.

But I never get the chance. A few months later, the County Attorney accepts Aden's plea to one felony and agrees to drop the other charges. The statutes of limitations will only allow punishment under the law as applied when the crime was committed, 1989. Aden will receive a maximum of forty-five days in jail and probation, but he won't have to register as a sex offender. I decline my right to request punitive damages or any financial compensation.

I can't bring myself to go to his first court appearance. Royal goes for me. She reports that forty-eight people show up to support him, so many that some supporters sat on the prosecution's side. They glared at her, shunning her merely for sitting in a courtroom. Some waited for her outside, she said, so she stayed inside until the last car left the parking lot.

We go to the plea hearing together. Aden looks just as I remember, except much older and smaller. His long, square beard has grayed. When he speaks, everything comes back to me. His deep voice makes me shudder, and all emotion leaves me. I feel just as stiff and removed as the proceedings that are unfolding around me.

THE COURT: Mr. Slabaugh, this is a new amended Count four of the formal complaint of criminal sexual conduct in the third degree, a felony-level violation under Minnesota Statute 21609.344 from incidents alleged to have occurred in Fillmore County, Minnesota, on or about February 13, 1989. To that charge, how do you plead: guilty or not guilty?

DEFENDANT: Guilty.

THE COURT: The Court has taken a plea of guilty from the defendant. Attorney Bauer, I'll now allow you to elicit factual basis to support his plea.

MR. BAUER: Thank you, Your Honor. Mr. Slabaugh, back in the spring of 1989, you were residing at …

SLABAUGH: Correct.

MR. BAUER: And that's located in Canton, Minnesota?

SLABAUGH: Correct.

MR. BAUER: And at the time, you would have been 27 years old that spring; is that correct?

SLABAUGH: Correct.

MR. BAUER: Your date of birth, in fact, is August 30th of 1961?

SLABAUGH: Correct.

MR. BAUER: Would you have had contact with an individual with the initials L.H. during that period of time?

SLABAUGH: I did.

MR. BAUER: And how did you know L.H.?

SLABAUGH: Pretty much grew up with her.

MR. BAUER: Okay. And at the time, L.H. was also working with you as kind of—as a—working at the farm with you; is that correct?

SLABAUGH: Correct.

MR. BAUER: And L.H.'s birth date was 7/26 of 1974?

SLABAUGH: I guess. I couldn't confirm that.

MR. BAUER: She, at the time, in the spring of 1989, would have been about 14½ years old?

SLABAUGH: Correct.

MR. BAUER: And that was your understanding. You knew that; is that correct?

SLABAUGH: Yes.

MR. BAUER: And during the spring of 1989, you had sexual contact and also sexual penetration with her; is that correct?

SLABAUGH: Correct.

MR. BAUER: You guys had sex on multiple—multiple—different occasions. But at least one of those occasions happened at your residence; is that right?

SLABAUGH: Correct.

MR. BAUER And at the time, she would have been 14 ½ and you would have been just over 27 years old?

SLABAUGH: Correct.

I sit with my hands clasped, numb. No one says the word "rape."

XX
August 2018

The backlash comes in threatening phone calls, handwritten letters, on social media, and in gossip all around me:

How dare you call it rape when we all know you asked for it?

We know it's all motivated by money.

There's no way you can be raped 26 times.

Absolutely no reason you should be able to drag him through the mud when he served his punishment thirty years ago. (The church shunned Slabaugh for 6 weeks in 1989, and then made him Deacon.)

You're causing other men in the community to sit on pins and needles because they don't know when they're going to be reported.

You have no idea how hated and unwanted you are in this community.

You're a slut.

You're a whore.

You do not want to meet me in a dark alley.

XXI
September 2018

i haven't finished writing my Victim Impact Statement, and I don't think I can read it when the time comes. I ask Royal if she will read it for me. She agrees, but a week before the sentencing, I still have only a jumble of angry paragraphs. I don't know for sure if Titus or the kids are coming. I don't know if I will be alone in the courtroom. Part of me doesn't want anyone to come. I don't want to put them in that position. It's my job as a mother to take care of others, not the other way around. But another part of me desperately wants my family there, so they will understand why I've been so overprotective over the years, never letting them have sleepovers, or not allowing them to be alone with certain relatives.

The prevailing rumors are that the Amish community has flooded the courthouse with calls and letters of support for Aden, as well as testimonies of my reputation (a "promiscuous," "ungodly liar") and theories of my motive (money). I hear whispers that the judge has already made up his mind that Aden will receive no jail time. I get warnings that his supporters will spill over to our side of the courtroom again. Royal asks if I'd let any of our friends know about the sentencing. I tell her I haven't. They have their own children, spouses, and jobs. Some live far away, and I haven't talked to them for months. I'm tired of talking about it. Most of all, I'm just tired.

Two nights before the sentencing, I have my outfit for court carefully picked out, ironed, and hanging in the closet. I make dinner for the kids and spend extra time cleaning up the kitchen. I sit on the sofa with my statement and stare at the scribbles and scratch marks. I get up to make tea, check on Darrel, and make sure the doors are locked. I decide it's a good time to organize the junk drawer, then the medicine cabinet. I adjust and readjust the sofa cushions, and

I clean out the wood stove. Finally, I fall asleep, the pages of the unfinished statement scattered over my lap.

Someone is talking to me. I open my eyes. Royal's round face smiles down at me. Faint light rims the edges of the curtains. Shadows still linger inside the house. "What time is it?" I ask.

"Four-thirty," she answers, as if we always wake up at this time. "Are you hungry?"

She doesn't wait for my answer. "I brought some friends." She bounces away, full of energy, and starts making noise in the kitchen. Other voices join her. I can hear the sounds of car doors slamming and people coming through the front door. I get up and walk through the hallway to the kitchen, still in my pajamas. There, women from various phases of my life bustle about, unpacking food and helping Royal with breakfast. One by one, they hug me, each expressing how grateful they are to be here.

These women, just like me, don't use the words I've heard for so long: "slut," "whore," "liar," "affair," "revenge." These women, who'd been taught only to obey and never question, use the words "rape," "brave," "grooming," "hero," "sexual predator," and "pedophile." I ask: "What are you all doing there? How did you know?"

"Royal called," they say, "yesterday."

"Yesterday?" I can't believe it. "How did you get here so fast?"

They made arrangements, jumped in cars, and drove through the night. I must look confused. "This is important, Lizzy," Royal says. I look at my sister. She's done it again, stepped in at the last minute to save my butt.

Our Amish blood is on display as we make a full breakfast and clean up by sunrise. One woman fixes my makeup while another furiously types up my Victim Impact Statement. Each woman has a story, and each of their stories reflects a piece of mine. Some of these women I've known from childhood; some are distant family I've reconnected with; some I've met through support networks. All of them escaped strict Amish and Plain communities. With two hours to go, we pile into a minivan and drive to the courthouse amid complete chaos. Someone in the back seat is still getting dressed, another putting on makeup. Everyone is talking over each other, their voices getting louder and faster as we approach the courthouse. Royal sits smooshed in the middle, quietly reading the statement.

We pull into the parking lot at 11:00 a.m., walk single file through the metal detector, and gather into a private conference room. Royal immediately shuts the blinds. Our friend, Mary, goes off to find a printer so Royal can read from a clean copy. We wait nervously, making small talk until the metal detector begins going off again. The high-pitched alarm sounds over and over, pausing only for a moment before ringing again. We look at each other. The Amish are here.

The door of the conference room opens, and I jump, half expecting to see a man in suspenders and a wide-brimmed hat holding a shotgun. But it's Rochelle. I hug her. "Thank you for coming," I whisper. Behind her, Titus stands sheepishly in the doorway. He's wearing a suit.

Mary comes running back into the room, statement in hand. "I need to look at this one more time," I say, "to make sure it's perfect or at least passable." I look down at the pages, unable to concentrate on the words. Rochelle reads over my shoulder. After a moment, she slips the first page out of my hand, picks up a pen, and starts making notes.

"This is good, Mom," she says. "It just needs a little fixing up." I watch her concentrating, occasionally making a note. She's all grown up, doing well in college, on her way to becoming an accountant. A wave of pride washes over me. Maybe we will be okay.

I'm shocked as more and more people arrive to show their support: members of our church as well as more men and women who've left nearby Amish and Mennonite communities. Just before 1:00 p.m., the deputy comes in to tell us that we're next. Royal suggests we pray. One by one, we clasp hands, spreading into a circle that wraps around the room. We bow our heads and Royal begins. "We ask you, Lord, for strength and courage today."

The room swells with energy. I can feel each person's hand in mine, Titus and Rochelle's on either side, as well as everyone else connected in the circle. I can feel their strength moving from hand to hand, arm to arm, seeping into my fingers and through my body. A powerful feeling slowly rises in my chest, pulling my shoulders back and raising my head—something like pride. I'm not sure. It's all new to me. "In Jesus's name, we pray."

The deputy opens the door and nods. It's time. Everyone looks at me one last time before filing out of the conference room. For a moment, Royal and I stand alone together. She has my Victim Impact Statement in her hands. I reach out to hug her once more. Royal presses the pages into my hands. "Lizzy, God spoke to me. And I'm sorry, but He told me this is not for me to read." Tears spring to my eyes. Royal puts her arms around me. "Lizzy, what are you so afraid of?"

I shake my head, dabbing my eyes with a tissue. "I'm not afraid, Royal," I say. "God spoke to me, too. I have to read it. I think I can do this."

"You are brave," Royal assures me.

The deputy holds open the door for us as we walk, arm in arm, into the courtroom. I can see Aden sitting with his back to us, the same square haircut, now gray and the wiry hair of his long beard still visible from the back of his head. I see his daughters in the back row, their ankles neatly crossed beneath their long, dark dresses, their heads bowed, patiently waiting. I can see our old neighbors, arms crossed, expressions grim. On the other side, dozens of friends and family and people from our church fill up the rows. I feel incredibly grateful to them just for being there. I grip the Impact Statement in both hands. Rochelle has positioned herself next to the podium, so she and Royal can stand beside me. I grab Royal's hand. She squeezes it back, then lets me go. I take the last few steps to the podium alone, take a breath, and begin to read:

Your Honor, I am sharing my story with you today because I was shamed into secrecy for 30 years. That secret is why we're here today. Aden and the Amish community are now hoping you will allow them to continue this secrecy for future generations. I have forgiven Aden and the Church that protected him, but I cannot forget the children I left behind. Seeking justice is my closure. I can't go back in time and tell the fourteen-year-old girl I was in 1989 that it wasn't her fault. I can't tell her that it wasn't okay for a man she trusted to rape her dozens of times. I can't tell her to come forward and seek justice. I can only do what's right today. I'm now doing everything I can to stop the cycle of abuse for my Amish brothers and sisters. Your Honor, I'm asking you today: Can you please help me?

Your Honor, I am trusting you to send a message that I couldn't: that no one is to blame for their rape. I believe that you can help me stop the cycle of abuse poisoning generations of Amish children. Healing can begin in this courtroom today if you use the power bestowed upon you to show that mercy belongs to the abused and not the abuser. I need your help to teach other victims that rape and shame are NOT just a part of growing up Amish. Even the night he raped me of my virginity, I didn't know it would change my life forever. Only now, looking back, I can see the damage he has done.

As an Amish child, I walked to a one-room schoolhouse in my bare feet. I felt guilty if I took a long break from my chores. I was taught I had no right to my own opinions, and I certainly had no knowledge of, or interest in, sex. I had never worn makeup, been to a party, had a boyfriend, tasted alcohol, or broken a curfew. I had never received any sex education. I didn't even know where babies came from because talking about it was forbidden. I was used to living with my own family and sharing a room with my sister. I dreamed of playing with baby kittens, not getting slammed into a wall and penetrated. I dreamed of learning to sew my own dress, not being raped in a buggy. I dreamed of exploring the mountains and getting good grades, not being shunned from the only life I'd ever known. I dreamed of someday falling in love and giving my virginity to my husband. All that ended the night Aden raped me.

At fourteen years old, I was denied a high school education and forced into modern slavery. Aden paid my parents a few dollars a week to live with him and his wife as their domestic servant. It was my job to wake up before dawn and help them take care of their home, four young children, and farm, until after dark. Aden's supporters would have you believe that at fourteen, I was a sophisticated homewrecker. To this day, they still call the rape an extramarital affair. Your Honor, I want to remind you I was not only a child and a virgin, I was too young to legally consent to anything, let alone sexual relations. Aden employed the classic grooming techniques of a child predator: presenting a wholesome image as a father and abiding community member. In secret, he used me for his sexual pleasure and discarded me when he was done. He put me at ease with a gentle and charming demeanor. But there was nothing gentle and charming about him during the rapes.

To this day, I am hurt by my family, friends, neighbors, and church community, both Amish and English, who knew about the abuse and did nothing to protect me. The state of Minnesota has never had a chance to protect me because it was considered a sin to speak to outsiders about Amish matters. And so, I was blamed, even by my parents. The adults responsible for me chose to protect the Amish church over the innocence of their own children.

The church still denies the existence of sexual abuse, despite the number of survivors coming forward. You can protect the next generation of Amish children from this devastating cycle of abuse. My Amish family deserve to maintain their way of life without the toxic legacy of abuse and secrecy. In some ways, it would have been easier to stay silent for another 30 years, but they created this secret, which made me physically, emotionally, and spiritually sick.

I've realized how many other Amish girls I'd left behind to be abused by men, like Aden, my uncles, and others in the community, who are protected by the church. I didn't want to report the rapes, but I knew I would never be free until I did. Your Honor, I believe that if you do the right thing, we can save future generations of Amish children from the same fate. I respectfully ask that you to send a message to Aden, the Amish community, and all sexual abuse survivors, that no one, especially a child, is responsible for their own rape. I guarantee there are people, still in the community today, who have been abused and who are suffering in silence. My hope is that you will tell them it is not their fault, that rape is a crime, and that there are people who care enough to protect them.

Judgment will be served by God, but protection needs to be served by the court. What is more worthy of justice than God's innocent children? Please help send a message to the Amish community that they are not alone, that they are worth all the protection we can provide. If the Amish community is not willing to protect their children, then we will. And to the Amish children, I want to say that you are not alone. I am with you, along with all the survivors here in the courtroom today. To us, you are worth the risk of coming forward. To us, you are worth all the justice in the world."

Acknowledgments

First of all, I'm grateful to each of my four unique children for giving me a purpose each and every day. Without you, I wouldn't have had a reason to delve so deep, to write my life story, and to pass on these words to my grandchildren, great-grandchildren, and so on. I love you all more than you will ever know.

Mother, I know you did the best you could in raising me, and I love and appreciate you for that.

Datt, I still miss you and your witty humor every day.

Gratitude goes to my sister for all the countless hours she has helped with this manuscript, with resources and information, with the website, and many other important details.

I love and appreciate all my four siblings and all of the cousins who I grew up with.

To my biological father and biological siblings, I want to meet each of you someday.

Special thanks go to my number one fans, Dr. Lars and Joni Johnson, for encouraging me on my journey. I have learned so much from your wisdom. You are both very special to me.

Sincere gratitude to everyone at the Fillmore County Police department and Marla Stanton with the District attorney's office.

Very special thanks to my cousin Rachel Yoder, author of *Nightbitch*, a novel. Rachel, you have been an inspiration to me. I appreciate all your help since we connected on 23 and me.

I'm especially thankful for my godparents, Brian and Mindy in the book, and their family for taking me on and helping me find my way in this huge new world. I'm forever grateful for your continued love and support. I know you always believed in me even when I didn't believe in myself.

Thank you to all my friends, whom I could always count on to read and sometimes reread many parts of the manuscript, for giving me honest feedback, and for asking me over and over, "When can we buy your book?"

To my friend, Susie, who inspires me to continue advocating to help others. High-five goes to her and her brother Aden (the 'amishpreneur') for helping me with the book title.

A big shout-out to Molly, my ghostwriter, editor, coach, and mentor for this book.

Huge thanks to Karyn at Nauset Press for believing in this manuscript, long before it was a book.

Much appreciation to Sherine Gilmour, Dr. Eric, and Renee Olson for proofreading the manuscript.

Thank you goes to Greg Schieber with Nethercut Schieber Attorneys, for all of his legal contributions.

Many thanks to all my beta readers, John and Lydia Schmid; Saloma Byler, author of *Why I left the Amish: A Memoir* (written with her pen name Saloma Miller

Furlong); Emma Gingerich, author of *Runaway Amish Girl: The Great Escape*; and Barbra Graber.

Last, but not least, thanks to each person that has positively impacted my life. I think of you often. Many of you are unaware of the incredible impact you left on me. I am grateful for each and every one of you who has prayed countless hours for me and my family.

Above all, to my savior Jesus Christ, to whom I give all my praise. He is the most important person to me today and always. He loves Lizzy completely for who she is, regardless of her past.

Resources

If you or someone you know is being abused, please reach out. The resources provided here were current at the time of publication.

A Better Way

Contact A Better Way for child abuse prevention information and education, assistance in reporting offenders to law enforcement, and victim support.

www.abetterway.org

hope@abetterway.org

Incest Aware

www.incestaware.org/

Suzanne Isaza

IncestAWARE@gmail.com

Plain Communities Task Force

Linda Crockett, Director, Safe Communities

313 W. Liberty St., Suite 242

Lancaster, PA 17603

Office: 717-560-9991

Cell: 717-572-6404

Lcrockett@safecommunitiespa.com2

RAINN National Sexual Assault Hotline

www.Rainn.org

800-656–HOPE

Stein Counseling & Consulting Services

571 Braund Street

Onalaska, WI 54650

(608) 785–7000

Transformation Counseling, LLC

Angel Jackson

1221 W. Whitehall Road

State College, PA 16801

814-952–9010

angel.transformation@comcast.net

Trauma-Informed Writing Services

Molly Maeve Eagan

www.Mollymaeve.com

Voices of Hope

Your story matters.

Voicesofhopewomen@gmail.com

www.voicesofhope.events/

Ten percent of all book profits will be donated to support and educate

Plain people communities.

Check our website for more information:

LifeBehindBlueCurtains.com

Lizzy's Biography

Lizzy Hershberger was raised by ultra-conservative Swartzentruber Amish in Minnesota. After coming forward about systemic abuse in her church, Lizzy became recognized as an expert on Amish culture, as well as an advocate, panelist, speaker, and Amish language interpreter, for victims of abuse. She is the co-founder of **Voices of Hope**, a national support network helping women to find their own voice. She volunteers with groups like **Victim Services**, and other groups working to improve the lives of women and children. Before running away, also known as "jumping the fence," Lizzy was a hired girl for local families and a teacher in a one-room schoolhouse. After giving up everything she grew up with, she got married and became a mother to four children, served as a school board member and as president of her children's 4-H Club, and she became a co-founder of a support group for parents. In 2018, she testified as an expert witness on the Amish for a wastewater case that resulted in substantial environmental improvements. Lizzy's story has been featured in *Cosmopolitan*, *Rochester Woman*, and other multimedia platforms and podcasts.

Molly's Biography

Molly Maeve Eagan was born and raised in Brooklyn, NY. She began her writing career as a crime reporter, and her unique ability to connect with interview subjects turned her into an award-winning investigative journalist. As a sexual assault survivor, she spent years in recovery before dedicating herself to helping other survivors find their voices and tell their stories. Molly is a writer, editor, and organizer, advocating for diverse groups of survivors from isolated religious communities to Hollywood casting couches.

Discover more at Mollymaeve.com.

A Word About Uncle Abe

In July 2018, the author and another family member went to the Fillmore County Sheriff's Office to report two uncles for sexual abuse of a minor. One uncle is depicted by Uncle Abe in this story. Uncle Abe denied the allegations, and the Fillmore County District Attorney declined to press charges because the alleged crime was beyond the statute of limitations. Uncle Abe is an active and respected member of the Amish church, as well as being a grandfather to over twenty grandchildren.